Preface

The seal hunt is a story of superlatives. It's about men who pushed themselves to the limits of human strength and endurance in one of the most unforgiving places on the planet. It's about the thousands of desperately poor sealers who risked everything, year after year, for barely enough cash to keep food on the table. It's about the rich and famous ice captains whose annual trips north added to their glory, and to their riches. And it's about a handful of large merchant firms who staked their own investments, but other men's lives, on the annual seal hunt. A few failed hunts could easily drive a merchant firm into bankruptcy, but this was nothing compared to the risks the sealers took—risks that became painfully and publicly evident during the spring of 1914.

This book is about the 1914 *Newfoundland* sealing disaster, and provides a background to the nature of the early twentieth-century seal hunt. Having worked as a writer and researcher at the Maritime History Archive for several years, I hope to share with readers my love for both archival materials and this province's rich seafaring history. I hope documents contained in the following pages—which include photographs, crew agreements, maps, logbooks, newspaper clippings, and telegraphs—will add a new dimension to understanding a well-known story from Newfoundland's past.

This book does not contain footnotes, but does draw on primary and secondary sources, and I owe a special debt of gratitude to those from whose work I have benefitted. A list of selected sources is provided at the end of the book, but some deserve special mention.

Cassie Brown (1919-1986) remains the authority on the *Newfoundland* disaster and anyone who has not done so should read her fascinating book *Death on the Ice*. Her writing and research materials were invaluable to the creation of this book. Dr. Shannon Ryan is widely considered a leading expert on the Newfoundland seal hunt and his book *The Ice Hunters: A History of Newfoundland Sealing to 1914* greatly informed my writing. I also highly recommend his *Seals and Sealers: A Pictorial History of the Newfoundland Seal Fishery.*

Most of my primary sources (excluding photographs) came from two archival collections: the Royal Commission of Enquiry into the Sealing Disasters of 1914 fonds at The Rooms Provincial Archives, and the Cassie Brown collection at the Archives and Special Collections Division of the QEII Library at Memorial University. All quotations from the *Newfoundland* survivor, Cecil Mouland, were transcribed from audiotapes of Brown's interviews with him. Quotations from the other survivors were extracted from their testimonies submitted to the Royal Commission. William Coaker's log is reproduced in this book as it appeared in the *Daily Mail* newspaper from April 11 to 17, 1914, although typographical, grammatical, and spelling errors have been silently corrected.

If errors have crept in, despite all the research and proofreading and fact checking that preceded publication of this manuscript, then they are my own. My fondest hope is that readers find this a compelling story and enjoy examining the images and documents that appear throughout this book.

Invitation to the Ice

The working life of the sealer was not something most politicians cared much about in 1914. The seal hunt, one of Newfoundland's oldest industries, had poured large sums of money into the public purse, but the government did little to regulate it. Instead, the seal hunt was controlled by the small group of men who profited the most from it—the merchants who owned the sealing ships and the ice captains who commanded them. Their assurances that the sealers were well looked after had satisfied most politicians—but not William Coaker.

Coaker was the leader of the newly formed Union Party, the first political party in Newfoundland to represent rural workers—sealers, fishers, and loggers. The party's first general election was in 1913, and eight of its nine candidates won their seats, including Coaker in Bonavista Bay.

During the House of Assembly's 1914 winter session, Coaker introduced a bill aimed at improving sealers' working conditions. It insisted that merchant firms provide better sleeping accommodations aboard the steamers, better food, and a doctor for each vessel. The Legislative Council passed the bill on March 11, 1914, but restricted it to the newer steel ships. The sealing fleet in 1914 consisted of 10 steel vessels and 11 wooden ones.

Sir William Coaker, n.d. *Archives and Special Collections Division (ASCD), Coll. 009 01.02.014*

Union Party members elected in the 1919 general election. *The Rooms Provincial Archives Division, VA 82-20.2*

Not content to simply write legislation from St. John's, Coaker wanted to experience the seal hunt first-hand. If he claimed to represent the sealers, then he should see how they worked. The merchant firm of Job Brothers offered him a place on the *Nascopie*, a powerful steel-hulled vessel built in 1911. Coaker invited his friend Charles Bryant to join him, and the two departed the port of St. John's on March 13. They spent the next four weeks in the North Atlantic ice floes observing how the *Nascopie*'s 271 sealers worked and lived.

Coaker kept a daily logbook of

The *Nascopie* at the icefields, ca. 1930. William Coaker went to the seal hunt aboard this steamer in 1914. *Maritime History Archive (MHA), PF-118.004*

his experiences, which was later serialized as "Mr. Coaker's Log" in the *Daily Mail* newspaper from April 11 to April 17, 1914. It is reproduced in its entirety in this book. Coaker's log provides a compelling eyewitness account of a turn-of-the-century seal hunt. It also records how he and the *Nascopie*'s sealers reacted to news of the *Newfoundland* disaster as it unfolded. The log remains important 100 years later because of its insight into Coaker, the seal hunt, and the *Newfoundland* disaster—all three have tremendous historical significance to the province.

After the 1914 seal hunt, Coaker helped create a Commission of Enquiry that would ultimately change the way the sealing industry was regulated.

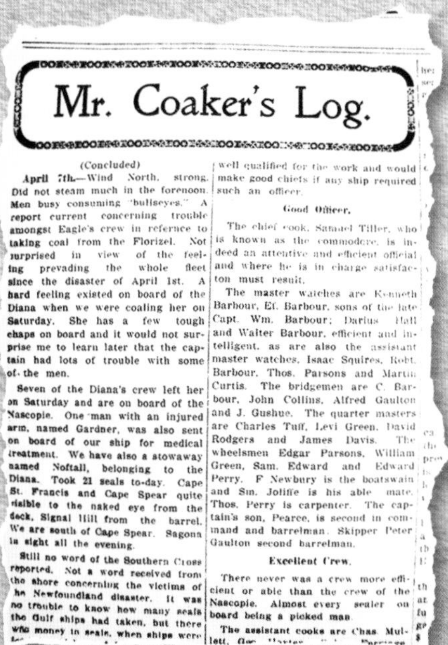

Mr. Coaker's Log.

(Concluded)

April 7th.—Wind North, strong. Did not steam much in the forenoon. Men busy consuming "bullseyes." A report current concerning trouble amongst Eagle's crew in refernce to taking coal from the Florizel. Not surprised in view of the feeling prevading the whole fleet since the disaster of April 1st. A hard feeling existed on board of the Diana when we were coaling her on Saturday. She has a few tough chaps on board and it would not surprise me to learn later that the captain had lots of trouble with some of the men.

Seven of the Diana's crew left her on Saturday and are on board of the Nascopie. One man with an injured arm, named Gardner, was also sent on board of our ship for medical treatment. We have also a stowaway named Noftall, belonging to the Diana. Took 21 seals to-day. Cape St. Francis and Cape Spear quite visible to the naked eye from the deck, Signal Hill from the barrel. We are south of Cape Spear. Sagona in sight all the evening.

Still no word of the Southern Cross reported. Not a word received from the shore concerning the victims of the Newfoundland disaster. It was no trouble to know how many seals the Gulf ships had taken, but there who money in seals, when ships were

well qualified for the work and would make good chiefs if any ship required such an officer.

Good Officer.

The chief cook, Samuel Tiller, who is known as the commodore, is indeed an attentive and efficient official and where he is in charge satisfacton must result.

The master watches are Kenneth Barbour, Ef. Barbour, sons of the late Capt. Wm. Barbour; Darius Hall and Walter Barbour, efficient and intelligent, as are also the assistant master watches, Isaac Squires, Robt. Barbour, Thos. Parsons and Martin Curtis. The bridgemen are C. Barbour, John Collins, Alfred Gaulton and J. Gushue. The quarter masters are Charles Tuff, Levi Green, David Rodgers and James Davis. The wheelsmen Edgar Parsons, William Green, Sam. Edward and Edward Perry. F Newbury is the boatswain and Sm. Joliffe is his able mate. Thos. Perry is carpenter. The captain's son, Pearce, is second in command and barrelman. Skipper Peter Gaulton second barrelman.

Excellent Crew.

There never was a crew more efficient or able than the crew of the Nascopie. Almost every sealer on board being a picked man.

The assistant cooks are Chas. Mullett, [illegible]

The *Daily Mail* published the journal Coaker kept of his 1914 voyage to the seal hunt. *Daily Mail, April 17, 1914*

William Coaker

William Ford Coaker was born on October 10, 1871. His father was a carpenter and sealer from Twillingate, and his mother was from St. John's. Coaker grew up on the Southside of St. John's, an area predominately populated by fishers and sealers. There he gained an awareness of the class divisions that separated the poor and powerless working class from the wealthy elite: the merchants, businessmen, and politicians.

Coaker rebelled against power structures early in life. When he was just 13 years old, he found part-time work as a fish handler for the merchant firm Job Brothers and almost immediately organized a strike to demand better wages. The merchant firm capitulated and Coaker discovered he had a gift for leadership and for rallying others to his cause.

But like many children of working-class parents, Coaker had to leave school at an early age so he could work full-time and help support his family. When he was 14, he became a clerk for the St. John's merchant firm of McDougall and

Templeton. He showed so much promise that he was promoted to manager of its Pike's Arm branch in Notre Dame Bay in 1887. By the time he was 20, Coaker had saved enough money to buy the branch, but he then lost everything in the bank crash of 1894.

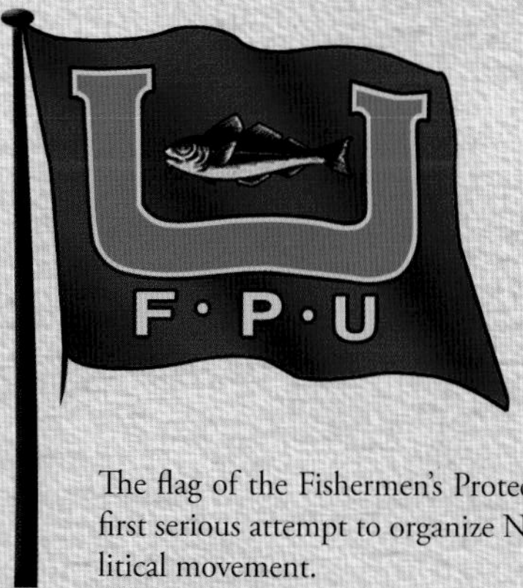

The flag of the Fishermen's Protective Union. The FPU was the first serious attempt to organize Newfoundland fishers into a political movement.

Coaker worked for a few years as a farmer and telegraph operator in Notre Dame Bay, where he became increasingly sympathetic to the plight of rural workers. Fishers and sealers were kept in a state of perpetual poverty, while merchant firms scooped up the bulk of all wealth produced by their labour. In 1908, Coaker formed the Fishermen's Protective Union (FPU) to represent working-class interests. It adopted the motto "To Each His Own."

Coaker was a gifted orator and the FPU steadily grew under his charismatic leadership. Its political wing, known as the Union Party, put eight men in the House of Assembly after the 1913 general election. Coaker was among those elected. The Union Party gave the working class unprecedented influence over political and economic affairs. Coaker continued to fight for the rights of the working class until his retirement in 1932. He died in 1938 at the age of 67.

The Fleet Departs

MR. COAKER'S LOG

FIRST INSTALLMENT OF MR. COAKER'S LOG OF THE VOYAGE OF THE STEAMER *NASCOPIE*.

March 13th — Grand March morning. Left St. John's at 8 a.m. being the fourth ship to pass the Narrows. Passed Baccalieu Island at 10:30 a.m., being first ship. Ice gradually becoming closer and heavier. Made good progress. All steel ships in sight at nightfall. *Adventure* last, about 10 miles from us. All foremost ships—*Stephano*, *Bellaventure*, *Florizel*, *Beothic* and ourselves together. Steamed half speed, as many large pieces of ice amongst the floe; considered too dangerous to proceed.

Spent night about 30 miles off Cape Freels. *Stephano* and *Nascopie* led whole day. Both splendid ships for forcing through close packed panned ice. Crew preparing gaffs and hauling ropes.

Passed several foxy bedlamer seals on ice. Very quiet. Saw smoke two wooden steamers in afternoon, both well in on the land and must find ice close packed.

Sealers line up with their gaffs as the fleet prepares to steam north, ca. 1900. *MHA, PF-001.1-A10*

Newfoundland's sealing fleet numbered 21 steamers in 1914. Every one of them was a household name. The *Nascopie* and seven other vessels departed St. John's on March 13. Most of the others, including the *Newfoundland*, left from more northerly ports—Wesleyville and Poole's Island. A few departed from Channel, on Newfoundland's southwest coast, bound for the Gulf of St. Lawrence seal hunt. Wherever the vessels departed from, they were cheered on by excited crowds. As the fleet steamed north, it carried with it the hopes and fortunes of the sealers' families and sometimes their entire communities. Outport households needed the spring seal hunt to supplement their meagre earnings from the summer fishery. A bad hunt could mean a hungry winter. Worse still was the threat of death.

It was a risk that Newfoundland sealers had been facing for generations. The commercial seal hunt dates back to the spring of 1793, when a St. John's merchant sent two small schooners to the North Atlantic ice floes to catch seals. When they returned with 1,600 pelts, an industry was born.

Soon, hundreds of vessels and thousands of men sailed to the floes annually. The contribution to Newfoundland's society and economy was enormous. Seal oil was an important lighting fuel and found a large market in Britain. Leather and furs were lucrative exports too.

The hunt also influenced settlement patterns. Until the late eighteenth century, Newfoundland was largely a summer home for European fishers who arrived annually

to catch cod. A commercial seal hunt gave them something to do in the off-season. It even used the same schooners that fished off the Grand Banks and Labrador coast. The outbreak of war in Europe during the late 1700s and early 1800s saw the price of Newfoundland cod skyrocket. Armed with two profitable industries that could employ the same people at different times of the year, Newfoundland attracted thousands of permanent settlers from England and Ireland.

By the 1830s, the seal hunt was booming. More than 300 vessels and 7,000 men sailed to the ice floes annually. They came from communities all along Newfoundland's north and east coasts, such as Greenspond, Twillingate, Fogo, and Catalina, but most sailed out of Conception Bay. St. John's also participated, but it was outport Newfoundland that truly flourished during the era of sail. Vessels were built, owned, and crewed locally. Many ports processed their own seal oil. At its peak, the industry accounted for about one-third of Newfoundland's exports.

The first steamers appeared at the floes in the 1860s. Large and powerful, they could penetrate deep into the icefields and bring back thousands of pelts. Unable to compete, the schooner fleet grew steadily smaller. The changes to the industry were profound. Power became concentrated in the few large merchant firms that could afford to buy expensive steamers. Most were based in St. John's. The steamer fleet employed fewer sealers than the schooners and men had to travel to St. John's to find a berth. The local shipbuilding industry also suffered because the steamers were foreign-built.

Soon, the once-mighty industry showed signs of decline. Petroleum had eclipsed seal oil on the international market and cut deep into Newfoundland's profits. In 1914, seal products accounted for a paltry 5 per cent of the island's exports. Nonetheless, a successful hunt could still make captains rich and add to the wealth of merchant firms. It could put much-needed cash in the hands of poverty-stricken sealers and their families. For this reason, hundreds of outport sealers annually risked their lives at the floes, while the spectators that bid them farewell in March anxiously awaited their safe return in April.

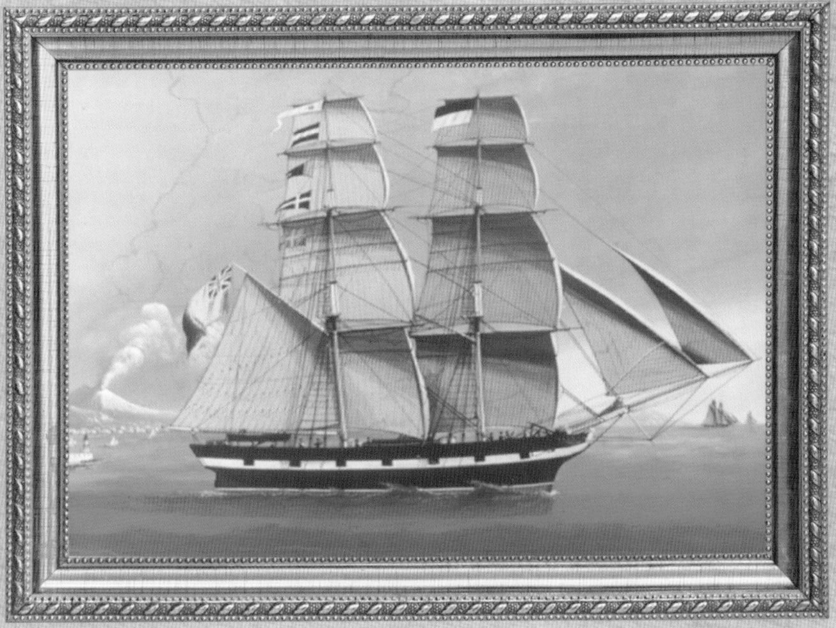

Sailing vessels like this brig dominated the seal fishery before the advent of steam in the 1860s.
MHA, PF-008.048

Vessel Profile: *Nascopie*

The SS *Nascopie* was one of the fleet's most powerful vessels in 1914. Weighing in at 1,004 tons, the steel-hulled icebreaker could carve its way through the icefields with far greater ease than the older wooden steamers, such as the 568-ton *Newfoundland*. It measured 186 feet long and 44 feet wide and carried 271 men to the icefields. Only two vessels were larger: the *Stephano* and *Florizel*. Built in 1911 at England, the *Nascopie* was co-owned by the Hudson Bay Company and the merchant firm Job Brothers. It prosecuted the seal fishery for four springs (1912-1915) before Job Brothers relinquished its share of the vessel. From then on, the *Nascopie* served as a supply ship for the Hudson Bay Company and operated primarily in the Hudson Strait and Arctic waters, although it returned for the 1927-1930 seal hunts (supplied by Bowring Brothers). In 1947 the steamer ran aground near Cape Dorset in the Canadian North, where stormy weather eventually broke it to pieces.

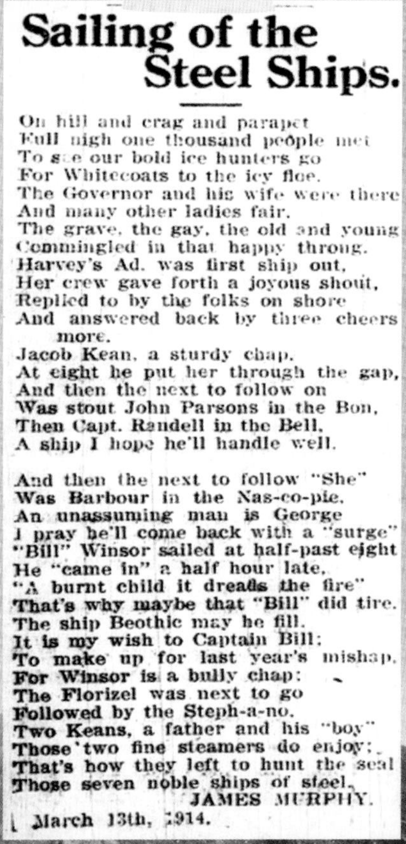

Sailing of the Steel Ships.

On hill and crag and parapet
Full nigh one thousand people met
To see our bold ice hunters go
For Whitecoats to the icy floe.
The Governor and his wife were there
And many other ladies fair.
The grave, the gay, the old and young
Commingled in that happy throng.
Harvey's Ad. was first ship out,
Her crew gave forth a joyous shout,
Replied to by the folks on shore
And answered back by three cheers more.
Jacob Kean, a sturdy chap.
At eight he put her through the gap,
And then the next to follow on
Was stout John Parsons in the Bon,
Then Capt. Randell in the Bell,
A ship I hope he'll handle well.

And then the next to follow "She"
Was Barbour in the Nas-co-pie.
An unassuming man is George
I pray he'll come back with a "surge"
"Bill" Winsor sailed at half-past eight
He "came in" a half hour late.
"A burnt child it dreads the fire"
That's why maybe that "Bill" did tire.
The ship Beothic may he fill.
It is my wish to Captain Bill;
To make up for last year's mishap.
For Winsor is a bully chap:
The Florizel was next to go
Followed by the Steph-a-no.
Two Keans, a father and his "boy"
Those two fine steamers do enjoy;
That's how they left to hunt the seal
Those seven noble ships of steel.

JAMES MURPHY.

March 13th, 1914.

Evening Telegram, March 13, 1914

The *Nascopie* at the ice floes, ca. 1930.
MHA, PF-118.002

INTO THE FLOES

MR. COAKER'S LOG

ICE HEAVY

March 14th — Ships began to move at daylight. Ice heavy and close; here and there streaks of water which two ships availed of. *Stephano* leading, with us very close after, most of the day. The *Nascopie* forged ahead two or three times and took the lead. At mid-day heaving ice was loose at Fogo. Ships headed for the land, and all the steel ships with the *Newfoundland* congregated about 10 miles off Fogo, all laying side by side. We took snap shot of the view.

Seeing no chance of getting North inside all resolved to force through Eastern. The *Bloodhound* was left at Shoal Bay where she probably laid up hoping the ice would pass out and leave clear water on the inside. The *Sagona* and *Eagle* were at Baccalieu Island, but the whole of Green Bay was a solid field of ice; not even a crack. The *Newfoundland* followed the steel ships as near as possible, but soon got far behind.

About 4:00 p.m. laid out of sight, we passed through quite a few hoods, as we also did earlier in the day before making in for the land. The body of hoods would now probably be about 40 miles N.E. of Fogo Islands. Some of the hoods had not pupped, although many families were passed. The hoods commenced to pup this year about the 12th and the pupping would extend to about the 17th.

We passed one white coat about 8 a.m., about 40 miles W.E. of Cape Fogo. The little chap was quite lively and we knocked him into the water in forcing through. He soon managed to mount the ice.

At nightfall all the steel ships were in two groups. One group about five miles Eastern of us, consisting of the *Florizel*, *Bonaventure* and *Adventure*; the other group consisted of *Stephano*, *Newfoundland*, *Beothic* and *Bellaventure*. The four ships laying within the radius of one hundred yards; the *Stephano* about thirty feet from us.

The appearance was more like a town than the Arctic Atlantic, as all the ships were brilliantly lighted. The ice very heavy and when the ships stopped it was impossible to proceed another foot. All decided to await developments that would likely present themselves at day-light.

Newfoundland's sealing steamers often travelled in packs at the icefields.
ASCD, Coll. 203 7.01.103

To find its catch, the Newfoundland sealing fleet had to steam into one of the most ferocious and unpredictable environments on the planet—the North Atlantic icefields. Also known as "The Front," it was a battleground where steamers and men had to defend against sudden blizzards, thrashing waves, fierce winds, and sea ice powerful enough to smash a steamer to pieces. The first to sink was the *Wolf* in 1871, crushed by an iceberg. By the time Coaker boarded the *Nascopie* in 1914, steamer losses had risen to 36.

But it was on these icefields that the Atlantic harp seal herds congregated each spring to give birth. Motivated by profit, the merchant firms gambled the cost of their vessels—and the lives of their employees—against the hope of bringing in a bumper crop. By late February, vast stretches of floating pack ice had appeared off southern Labrador and northeastern Newfoundland. It included coastal ice that winds and tides had carried offshore and the large Arctic floes that travel south on ocean currents. The ice pack sometimes made it as far south as the Grand Banks before retreating north in the late spring.

was also advantageous
teamers to clear from a
ser to the icefields than

ers typically stayed at
ur to six weeks before
land. They usually de-
March and returned by
, although some did not
y May.
leet cleared port between
13. The *Diana* was the
n May 3. It once would
nal for the steamers to re-
s for a second trip, but
lland government out-
tice in the 1890s to pro-
from over-exploitation.
nt also determined the
unting season each year.

n any other
ute the seal
vessel, and
he *Stephano*

nd sank the
e. American

The iron-clad *Stephano*. *MHA, PF-001.1-Q23b*

Vessel Profile: *Newfoundland*

The *Newfoundland* was considerably older, weaker, and less maneuverable than the *Stephano*. Built at Quebec in 1872, the wooden-wall measured 212 feet long and 29 feet wide, and weighed 568 tons. It had been prosecuting the Newfoundland seal fishery since 1893, in both the North Atlantic icefields and the more tranquil Gulf of St. Lawrence. Westbury Kean, Abram's youngest son, had been the *Newfoundland's* captain since 1911. After the 1914 disaster, A. Harvey and Company sold the *Newfoundland* to the merchant firm Job Brothers. The vessel was renamed the *Samuel Blandford* and returned to the hunt for one more voyage in 1916. In August of that year it became shipwrecked on rocks in St. Mary's Bay.

The wooden-wall *Newfoundland*.
ASCD, Coll.115 16.04.099

Ice Everywhere

MR. COAKER'S LOG

OFF AGAIN AT DAYBREAK

March 15th (Sunday) — Our fleet started at daybreak. *Florizel*, *Bonaventure* and *Adventure* away to S.E., about ten miles; *Newfoundland* about eight miles distant nearer to the land. Apparently *Newfoundland* intends to hold on for hoods—a wise decision as it ought not to be hard to make up 20,000 hoods, old and young, especially in view of having guns to kill the old dogs. We passed through ice containing several families in the early part of the day.

The *Stephano* leading our fleet, following leads of water, which carried us to all parts of the compass. Wind W.S.W., strong, which caused the leads of water. *Florizel* and her associates apparently jammed; we passed out of sight at about 2 p.m. At nightfall supposed to be thirty miles East of Groais Island. The ocean one solid mass, not a drop of water visible. The four ships in our fleet again berthed together, almost side by side for another night.

Word from Fogo assures us that inside ships still unable to get North. Not a wave of sea, the ocean one solid mass of heavy ice. Impossible to make headway by butting; can only follow leads and cracks if such occur occasionally.

CREW ENJOY THEMSELVES

Crew happy enjoyed their fresh beef and figgy pudding for dinner, fish and brewse for breakfast, was excellent. For tea they had soft bread and canned beef. Men in hold singing hymns all day. Some held free and easy Methodist service after tea, which went off as just though they were in a church building. The order was perfect.

Captain thinks we are about thirty miles from seals. Too bad other three ships should have been nipped and thereby delayed. *Beothic* lost blade of propellor.

March 16th — The four ships in our company started together. Ice close, and a solid field. A few lakes of water which ships tried to follow. Did not make much progress. At nightfall about twenty miles East of Groais Island.

CLOSE TOGETHER

The four ships spent the night close together, the *Beothic* being a very close neighbour. The *Stephano* was leading most of the day. Some of the ships gave considerable trouble owing to keeping too close to the sterns of the leading ships, which made insufficient space for backing when hard knots are encountered. Some of the ships barely escaped being damaged today owing to this incessant practice which is anything but desirable or satisfactory.

Reports state ships inside still jammed, and the balance of the steel fleet with the *Sagona* about ten miles north of Fogo. A splendid day.

Chopping up ice to free a jammed steamer. *City of St. John's Archives, 8.01.011*

Only the most skilled seafarers could navigate the treacherous ice-choked waters that awaited them at the Front. The icefields were a vast and frozen frontier of tightly packed white ice interlaced here and there with narrow veins of water known as "leads." Steamers tried to follow a lead of water as deeply into the floes as possible to find the seal herds. Failing this, they tried to forge their own paths by breaking the ice—riding up on it and cracking through or simply ramming into the floes head-on.

Nothing about this work was safe. Every species of ice populated these waters: from the giant bergs that could crush a 20,000-ton ocean liner to the many smaller chunks of floating ice that were difficult to see but still powerful enough to punch a hole in a steamer's hull. If sealing crews were inexperienced, inattentive, or just plain unlucky, they risked losing their vessels and even their lives.

It was the scunner's job to guide the vessel through the icy water. This crewmember stood in a barrel mounted high on the vessel's foremast and shouted directions to the wheel crew below. A good scunner could thread the vessel through the thickest floes; a bad one would get wrecked in the thinnest crust of ice. The sealers took turns in the barrel, and only the captain could override the scunner's orders.

Becoming trapped in tight ice was one of the hunt's most frequent problems. A jammed vessel could not reach the lucrative seal herds and pressure from the pack ice threatened to damage its hull. More than one vessel sank while jammed at the floes. Fortunately, ice that was tight enough to crush a steamer could also support the weight of the sealers on board. The men would have to abandon ship and hope that another crew soon spotted them. Rescue

No. 2 "Florizel Series".
S. S. "Florizel" at Icefields - Ship goes clear.

The Rooms Provincial Archives Division, A 30-66

was certain while the steamers travelled close to one another, but the icefields were large and the steamers did not always travel in packs.

The sealers worked hard to free a jammed vessel. They jumped and stomped on the ice and chopped at it with axes, usually getting drenched with freezing water in the process. Ropes were thrown overboard and the men tried to drag the vessel forward. Engines thrashed the vessel back and forth and its hull gnashed at the ice around it. An effective method was to blast the vessel clear with gunpowder, brought to the icefields by the barrelful for this purpose. A first-hand account of this dangerous strategy appears in the diary of 17-year-old A. Stanley Harvey, grandson of the prominent clergyman and naturalist Moses Harvey, who went to the icefields in 1908 as a passenger aboard the steel-hulled *Bloodhound*:

"The process of getting her off is rather interesting. First, powder is put into bottles and then the fuse is set alight. It is then shoved down into the ice (through a hole chopped) by means of poles. After a breathless wait we hear a rumble and the ice cracks sometimes a couple of hundred yards, then with a roar great blocks of ice are hurled with terrific force through the air, everybody yells out 'heads in under,' meanwhile we scatter here and there to evade the falling ice, it is very exciting. When all is over long poles are thrown from the ship until every man has one, then all the slob ice is passed along the ship into her wake, the engines are reversed and if she moves, the rope from her bow is dropped over and everyone catches hold and pulls her through, if she fails to break the barrier, the process is repeated."

If the vessel was freed, it continued to hunt for the seals by either finding or creating another lead of water. It was also common for steamers to travel in groups so that the weaker vessels could take advantage of the leads opened up by the more powerful steamers in the fleet. This was a good strategy for penetrating the floes but introduced another risk: with so many large steamers trying to navigate the same narrow vein of water, collisions were difficult to avoid. It also must have galled an ice captain to open up a lead of water only to guide his rivals to the same patch of seals. It was the captain's job to find the seal herds and there was stiff competition to bring home the largest catch.

Captain George Barbour

Captain George Barbour was one of the most experienced and successful in the fleet. An ice master since 1893, he had already commanded six sealing steamers before taking on the mighty *Nascopie* in 1912. By then, Barbour had four times won the prestigious title of high liner for bringing home the most pelts in 1902, 1907, 1909, and 1911. A sealer who served under George Barbour knew he had a good shot at a big payday. Barbour spent 36 consecutive springs at the ice floes. He made his final voyage in 1928, before he died the following August.

ASCD, Coll. 203 5.14.002

The Vocabulary of the Hunt

The sealer's word-stock was large and lively—and confusing to outsiders and newcomers.
ASCD, Coll. 203 7.01.057

The seal hunt had a language all its own, a vibrant lexicon filled with terms like ice hunter, seal meadow, master watch, nunny bag, and gaff—phrases that may have intimidated or confused an outsider, while at the same time uniting the sealers into the family of the fleet. The vocabulary emerged to describe every aspect of the hunt: its methods, equipment, and personnel; the seals and their habits; and the multitude of sea ice and weather conditions that the sealers encountered. Some terms were unique to the hunt (e.g., ice hunter and whelping ice), others were borrowed and adapted (e.g., gaff).

The *Dictionary of Newfoundland English* (*DNE*) gives an idea of just how many words are associated with the hunt. The noun *seal* is one of its single largest entries (perhaps second only to *fish*) and sprawls across five pages. There are five alternate spellings—sile, soil, swale, swile, and swoil(e)—and dozens of word combinations, including seal finger (a disease common among sealers), seal meadow (the ice where seals congregate to give birth), seal pan (a pan of ice where sealers have piled their pelts), seal patch (a concentration of seals on the ice), and seal vat (the container used to render seal oil).

MR. COAKER'S LOG

March 17th — The four ships started early but found ice rafting and very tight. It took all day up to 3 p.m. to get clear of a sheet across which lay a lake of water. The *Bellaventure* got across our bow.

BOTHERED EACH OTHER

The four ships were working almost within a space of two hundred feet side by side. We had to go astern to allow the *Stephano* to come astern and by so doing our ship got nipped in a rafter. The other ships escaped the rafter but the three of them also became immovable. It took us until 6 p.m. to get clear of the position we were forced into owing to the *Bellaventure* getting in our way.

The other three ships went on West about eight or ten miles. We followed and at 8 p.m. when we had to "burn down," the other ships were a mile or two distant also "burned down."

It was too risky to venture further into field ice in the dark as it might mean being nipped in a heavy sheet, so the Captain wisely decided to "burn down," in a lake of water and await tomorrow morning's developments.

The day was an ideal one. Not cold, but clear, and very moderate. This is our fifth night at sea, and each night has found the ships "burnt down" and others of our fleet in close proximity.

We took a couple of good photos when the ships were jammed today as the crews were mostly engaged in attempting to do what was possible to set them free.

CREW WORKED WELL

Our crew worked well and, but for blowing up the ice to the windward of the ship it would have been impossible to proceed.

Our ship is out of trim being too much by the stern and all on board who sailed in her last spring say she is not near as good in heavy ice as she was then.

Complaints reached me last night from the *Beothic*, *Stephano* and *Bellaventure* about food. The *Stephano* did not supply brewse as by law provided. Neither did the *Bellaventure*, and in addition the *Bellaventure* did not supply fresh beef on Sunday. The same complaint is made of the *Beothic*.

I marconied the owners and trust their action will remove all grounds for future complaint; if not, owners and masters are responsible for the breaches of the law and may be sued before the courts.

The crew of the *Nascopie* are quite satisfied with the food which is fully up to the requirements of the new sealing law.

The dictionary devotes another four pages to the verb *seal* and to words that begin with seal—sealer, sealing, and sealskin. There are many word combinations under *sealing*: sealing ground (see seal meadow), sealing rope (used to haul pelts across the ice), and sealing season (when the seals migrate past Newfoundland), to name a few. Even the name of the commercial enterprise had its variants—it was a seal hunt, a seal fishery, and a sealing adventure.

Ice is another large entry in the *DNE* that contains many terms derived from the hunt. The sealers and sealing masters were known as ice hunters, ice pilots, ice captains, and ice skippers. The sealers formed an ice party and carried ice poles (or gaffs) to kill seals and keep their balance on unsteady ice pans. The men also used frosters, sparables, and chisels to help them walk across slippery ice—these were nails driven into boot soles. The hunt itself was ice work or ice fishing and the annual spring trip north an ice voyage into the icefields.

Many words existed in the sealer's vocabulary to describe sea ice. Small icebergs could be rolling pans, rollers, barricados, or clumpers. The most notorious were growlers because they were unpredictable, difficult to see, and powerful enough to sink a steamer. Large icebergs were known as islands of ice and their peaks pinnacles.

The seals had different names depending on their age. Harp seal pups were called cats or whitecoats and became raggedy jackets when their adult fur started to grow in. Seals old enough to swim were called beaters and those nearing breeding age were bedlamers. Adult females were called bitches, and the males dogs. The word *dog* had a second meaning—it was also the name for sealers who accompanied and carried gunpowder for the expert marksmen hired to shoot bedlamers and adult seals.

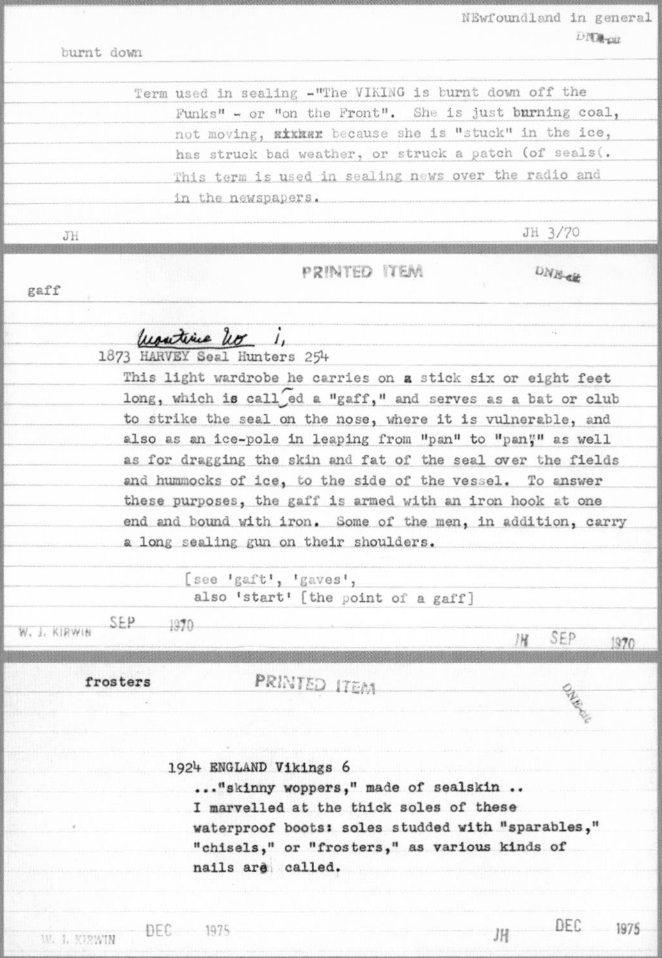

Reproductions of word files compiled by the editors of the *Dictionary of Newfoundland English. Reproduced with the permission of Memorial University's English Language Research Centre*

NEwfoundland in general
DNE
burnt down

Term used in sealing -"The VIKING is burnt down off the Funks" - or "on the Front". She is just burning coal, not moving, ~~xixkxx~~ because she is "stuck" in the ice, has struck bad weather, or struck a patch (of seals(. This term is used in sealing news over the radio and in the newspapers.

JH JH 3/70

PRINTED ITEM DNE
gaff

Wonderful Wo 1,
1873 HARVEY Seal Hunters 254
This light wardrobe he carries on a stick six or eight feet long, which is called a "gaff," and serves as a bat or club to strike the seal on the nose, where it is vulnerable, and also as an ice-pole in leaping from "pan" to "pan," as well as for dragging the skin and fat of the seal over the fields and hummocks of ice, to the side of the vessel. To answer these purposes, the gaff is armed with an iron hook at one end and bound with iron. Some of the men, in addition, carry a long sealing gun on their shoulders.

[see 'gaft', 'gaves', also 'start' [the point of a gaff]

W. J. KIRWIN SEP 1970 JH SEP 1970

frosters PRINTED ITEM DNE

1924 ENGLAND Vikings 6
..."skinny woppers," made of sealskin ..
I marvelled at the thick soles of these waterproof boots: soles studded with "sparables," "chisels," or "frosters," as various kinds of nails are called.

W. J. KIRWIN DEC 1975 JH DEC 1975

Not surprisingly, sealers had many words and phrases to describe sea ice. *MHA, PF-323.025*

Other words described the sealing steamers. When Coaker wrote that the *Nascopie* was "burnt down," he meant that the vessel had reduced the fire in its engine to stop in one place. A vessel might burn down to pass the night or after becoming jammed in ice.

Night was one of the few times a sealer stopped working and returned to his makeshift living quarters between decks, known as the dungeon. This was not the same as his berth, which referred to his position as a sealer on the vessel with a share in the hunt's profits. Sealers had to apply to merchant firms for berths aboard their vessels, which were typically awarded around Boxing Day.

On rare occasions, some or all crewmembers refused to work altogether and "manussed." Manussing was a form of non-violent protest and the word appears to have been unique to Newfoundland. It was usually aimed at ending a long and unsuccessful sealing voyage, but other factors could also prompt a crew to manus. In 1914, orders to continue sealing in the immediate wake of the *Newfoundland* disaster sparked manussing aboard four vessels: *Stephano*, *Bloodhound*, *Diana*, and *Eagle*.

FIRST DAY ON THE ICE

MR. COAKER'S LOG

DID GOOD WORK

March 18th — The *Stephano*, *Beothic* and *Bellaventure* were a few miles ahead in the morning but the *Nascopie* was not asleep. Soon Groais Island appeared out of the fog which prevailed. We sighted the three aforenamed ships and all raced for Cape Bauld in open water along the Treaty Shore. Captain Barbour decided to cut off South of Belle Isle as the ice appeared heavy. Soon the hulls of other ships in our fleet appeared heading South having gone as far as Cape Bauld and receiving information.

We were now seven or eight miles ahead; leading to the East. The other ships had some difficulty in getting through. At 3 p.m. we ran into the patch of white coats when about ten miles South of Belle Isle. The patch seemed to run North and South and the young seals looked large. It was our first sight of the white coats and everybody on board was intensely excited.

ALL STOOD READY

The men all stood by, with gaffs and hauling ropes ready to jump. We passed through this streak of seals which no doubt came South West of Belle Isle.

On and on the *Nascopie* went to the East. The other ships apparently were steaming about South East and were about seven or eight miles further South than the *Nascopie*.

About 5 p.m. we ran into quite a patch and the ship was stopped and all hands ordered on the ice for a tow of seals; all returned by dark, some with a few, with two and most all with three.

The slaughter had begun and in about an hour five hundred young seals were on board.

I weighed quite a number and they averaged fifty-four pounds. One weighed seventy-five pounds. They were indeed a prime lot of seals.

The ship then proceeded East and "burned down" about 8 p.m. with white coats crying in all directions.

IMPRESSIVE SOUNDS

The crying of a herd of white coats is something not easily to be forgotten. It resembles the cry of a thousand sea gulls when disturbed. It is a pitiable cry and it seems hard to slaughter those innocents. They are so purely white in appearance and so harmless. Just a tap on the nose with a gaff ends their life instantaneously. They are so round and fat.

They realize their danger. The old race about the ice in all directions tossing their heads erect, splurging into their blowing holes, then with a splurge they throw themselves once again on the ice and rush towards their crying babies. Some of them stand by their young and lose their lives in protecting their babes who are consistently crying to their mothers.

KNOW ITS OWN

Each mother seal knows the cry of its young just as well as a human mother would. Very few dog harps are taken for they always make off and escape into the blowing holes or in rents in the ice.

We found this whelping ice all broken up owing to having come in contact with Belle Island.There was not a wag of sea.

We took the first seals about twenty miles S.E. of Belle Island.

The *Stephano* and *Beothic* struck the patch about seven miles South of us. Learning we had struck the seals although the seals were not plentiful, they steamed towards us and when we "burned down" we were not more than two miles from the *Stephano* and *Beothic*.

A watch prepares to go overboard. *ASCD, Coll.115 16.04.011*

By the time the *Nascopie* reached its first patch of seals on March 18, only a few hours of sunlight remained for hunting. Such a short day on the ice would be unusual now that the vessel was in the fat. As long as there were seals and daylight, there would be work on the floes. The men might occasionally return to the vessel for some tea and bread during the day, but only if the *Nascopie* was within walking distance—a rare occurrence in the era of steam.

Steamers carried large crews, usually between 130 and 270 men, divided into smaller sealing parties known as watches. A vessel typically dropped off its first watch at daybreak and then steamed away to deposit other watches elsewhere among the floes. This gave the crew greater access to the massive seal herds, but it also meant that the men were rarely within walking distance of their vessel.

Sometimes watches from competing vessels worked within eyesight of each other and sometimes a steamer might pass by, but the icefields were vast and the seal herds immense, so more

A pan of seals. *MHA, PF-320.006*

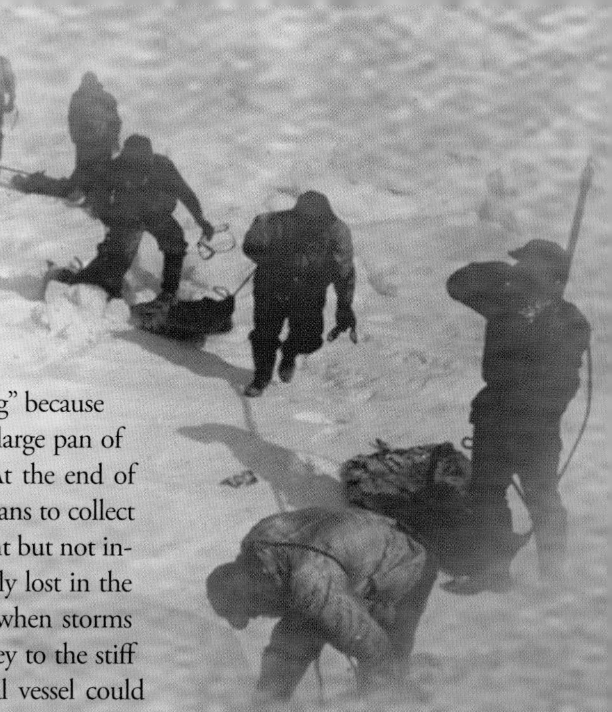

often than not the men worked in isolated groups. Sealers could spend 12 hours or more on the ice before their vessel returned to pick them up. It was a dangerous practice.

After the men scrambled down the side of their vessel, they walked across the ice pans to the seals. Sometimes they had to travel great distances as they hunted; other times they worked in a dense patch of seals. At all times they faced the threat of sudden storms and fog patches that could separate them from their crewmembers and their vessel. Even when the weather was good, a false step on an unsteady ice pan could send an unlucky sealer into the freezing waters.

The men killed seal pups with gaffs and the adults with guns. Almost all sealers hunted whitecoats and a single blow to the head could kill a pup instantly. Only expert marksmen were allowed to kill the adult seals because anything more than one shot to the head would damage the pelt.

Sealers usually removed the pelts on the ice and attached them to tow ropes. The pelt included the fur, fat, and one flipper. It weighed about 50 pounds. Sealers threaded about seven pelts onto a rope and dragged them across the jagged ice to a designated drop-off point. After the men piled up their pelts, they returned to hunt more seals.

This process was called "panning" because the drop-off point was usually a large pan of ice marked by the vessel's flag. At the end of each day, the steamer visited its pans to collect the pelts. The strategy was efficient but not infallible. A pan could become easily lost in the icy maze of the floes, especially when storms and fog moved in. Others fell prey to the stiff competition of the hunt—a rival vessel could easily scoop up pelts from an unguarded pan if its captain was unscrupulous or desperate.

Twelve cold hours on the ice were followed by even more work after the sealers returned to their vessel. Hundreds and sometimes thousands of pelts had to be hoisted on board and properly stacked on the deck, with fat pressed against fat and the skins facing out. Four hours was a good night's sleep to the sealer, if he could manage it. At daybreak, he would be on the floes again, hauling rope and gaff and jumping from pan to pan.

The Sealer's Kit and Clothing

The sealers lived and worked in one of the most extreme environments on the planet, yet they packed few items for their annual trip north.

A well-dressed sealer's outfit generally consisted of a canvas jacket, wool sweater, tweed or moleskin trousers, long underwear, mittens, a cap, and sealskin boots with studded soles. Some wore goggles to guard against the bright sun and ice. But the sealers were poor and even this outfit would have been too elaborate for many. It was not unusual for sealers to board a vessel wearing torn and flimsy clothing and jackets made from flour bags. Hats and mittens were luxury items.

Each sealer also packed his own equipment, which consisted of a gaff for killing seals, a knife for skinning carcasses, a piece of steel to sharpen the knife, and a tow rope for hauling pelts. The gaff was a 2-metre-long wooden pole with a spike and iron hook fastened to one end. It was invaluable to the sealers, who used it to balance themselves on the ice, to jump from pan to pan, and to rescue other sealers after they had slipped and fallen into the water.

Most sealers brought their own food to the ice because they could not always return to the vessel for snacks. This food was carried in a canvas or sealskin knapsack called a nunny bag. Hard bread was a staple and many sealers also carried oatmeal and raisins, which they mixed with melted ice. The men supplemented this meagre diet with seal hearts and livers, which they attached to their belts after killing a seal and ate raw or frozen. Seal blood provided a warm drink on the floes.

1898 *Greenland* Disaster

MR. COAKER'S LOG

March 19th — All were moving at 4:30 a.m. At five the ships steamed out further Eastern and placed the different watches on the ice; one watch mixed with men from the *Stephano* and the *Stephano*'s flags were mixed with the *Nascopie*'s at one section.

The men cleaned up the seals where they had been placed. The ship kept picking up the seals and replacing the men. This continued all day. My chum—C. Bryant—and myself went on the ice, with the men after dinner and although the seals were not plentiful and were cleaned up within two hours, Bryant killed, sculped and piled fourteen, and I had nine for myself. It was an experience to kill those little innocents pleading so pityfully for their lives, and the sculping of them was even sadder. I should say they contain fully sixteen pints of blood. I examined some hundreds of them during the day and the result of my investigations showed that about twenty-five per cent only were female. They had subsisted from birth entirely upon their mother's milk and their stomachs contained a large quantity of milk. I examined scores of the stomachs of the mother seals and found all without a particle of food and many of the stomachs contained large numbers of small worms. Many of the udders of the mother seals contained no milk. They appeared to be drying up the milk supply.

I doubt whether any of the prime full grown white coats would be nursed another three days by the mothers. I should think that those seals would be full-grown about the 20th and would not gain much in weight after that date. The younger seals, of course, would probably continue to suck for another week. But seals—such as seven-eighths of those taken by us—would certainly not grow much more this season.

They were probably pupped about March 1st and are about twenty days old. If they weighed fifteen pounds at birth some of them increased in weight eighty-five pounds in twenty days—that is carcass and pelt. The pelts averaged fifty-five pounds today, some went seventy-five, several sixty-eight.

I only weighed one at forty pounds. The carcasses weigh about twenty-five pounds for a pelt weighing sixty. The blood another ten pounds, which brings some up to a gross weight of ninety-five to one hundred pounds.

The pelt of the mother seal will average about one hundred pounds—so while a young harp at fifty-six pounds is worth $2.25, the mother weighing seventy pounds is worth but $3.00 to the sealers. During the afternoon it closed in foggy and looked as if it might snow. The men working in our section numbering sixty, all gathered at one place.

The sealing steamers *Greenland* (foreground) and *Vanguard*. In 1898, 48 of the *Greenland*'s crew froze to death in a blizzard while stranded on the ice. At least two of the survivors—George Tuff and Ezra Melendy—were aboard the *Newfoundland* in 1914. Tuff survived the 1914 disaster, but Melendy did not. *ASCD, Coll. 203 3.105.001*

Long before 1914, Newfoundland sealers had grown accustomed to death and disaster. One of the industry's worst tragedies took place in 1898, when 48 men from the *Greenland* froze to death after a sudden blizzard. The vessel was under the command of Captain George Barbour, master of the *Nascopie* in 1914.

In the early hours of March 21, 1898, Barbour distributed four watches among the ice floes. When a storm broke out that evening, he hurried to pick them up. The first watch made it on board at about 6 p.m., but by then winds and waves had packed the ice into a single impassable sheet. At the same time, a giant lead of water had opened up around the approximately 150 sealers still on the ice. They could not cross the water to reach their vessel and the *Greenland* could not penetrate the tight ice to save its men.

The blizzard was fierce and raged well into the next day. At about 4 p.m., search parties could finally take to the ice. They found most of the survivors, but a second storm halted their efforts later that night. Six more survivors made it to the *Greenland* the next morning, but 48 men never returned. Only 25 bodies were found.

Panning seals. Some survivors of the G
ter said they were forced to continue
weather because rival crews had stolen
unguarded pans of pelts. Although nothi
many sealers blamed the crew of the *Auro*
ed by Abram Kean. *City of St. John's Archi*

Back in Newfoundland, news
aster sparked early rumblings
tent with the way that govern
merchant firms regulated the se

The Evening Telegram, St. John's, Newfoundland.

DEATH ON THE ICEFIELDS.

SHOCKING and AWFUL DISASTER

TO THE "GREENLAND'S" HARDY CREW.

48 BRAVE MEN PERISH

TWENTY-FIVE DEAD BODIES BROUGHT IN.

MANY FROSTBITTEN—SOME VERY BADLY.

Details of the Terrible Calamity,

TOGETHER WITH NAMES OF VICTIMS.

PARTICULARS Of the Fatal Trip.

The Different Patches.

Could be Faintly Heard.

Laid Down to Die.

Killed and Panned

Assisted in the Rescue.

Put Out All His Men.

List of the Dead.

THE HEROES Of Our Frozen Pans DIE IN HARNESS While Battling for Bread FOR THEIR BABES.

The Harrowing Details

White and Anxious Faces

Icy Breath of Boreas.

A Sad Sight.

Sympathy With the Bereaved Relatives.

Ringing and Lusty Cheers?

THE EVENING TELEG

MR. COAKER'S LOG

NO SHIP IN SIGHT

here was no sign of the steamer. he *Bellaventure* was not far dis- nt and was picking up her men hich were well scattered. Some the older men thought we ght not be picked up before r 10 p.m. A punt was left by steamer as a mark to find the if it was late before we could eached. Some men housed in punt which had been placed her gunnall and which pro- d shelter from the wind. A vas made from flag poles, seal and carcasses.

me of the men played a called cat, which consisted king a seal flipper with a d then running to the next not struck with the flipper bowler.

ers began telling of their ears' experience at the ice thers who had survived m that had taken the lives eight of the *Greenland's* d of their terrible experi- hat blizzard.

—James Harris, of Har- ace—sang one of those oned witty songs which d the singer to dance at of each verse. Skipper bition brought down at the close and a er was given him when shed. Although about miles S.E. of Belle out on the bosom hty Atlantic Ocean's d with little hope of ship before eight or vening and with the of a snow storm, yet arts were full of life sm. A smile might be seen on the countenances of each.

Their faces were painted with blood which squirted from the beating arteries of the day's victims.

SPLENDID FELLOWS

A better company of men would be hard to find. Each of them this trying day had proved to be a man in a man's place—for a man must be a man when slaughtering white coats. He works as he never before worked unless he has been fortunate enough to have been in the white coats before.

Just at dark our ship appeared and soon she was alongside of our pan, and a rush was made for the side sticks and ladders which presented a sight impossible to comprehend unless viewing it on the spot.

How I wish it was light enough to secure a snap shot. The whole side of the ship was covered with black objects with faces all looking upwards, each pushing his gaff before him and an occasional back carrying a "cat white coat" slung across the shoulder. We had gone on the ice without any food as we had expected to be on board of the ship an hour after we left her. I was delighted with my first experience with the white coats and was well repaid for the inconveniences we had endured.

We did not make a good day's work for the seals were too scarce and scattered but when all we panned is on board we won't be far short of eight thousand seals.

The *Adventure* came in sight just before dark,—five thousand three hundred on board.

A List of Crew

MR. COAKER'S LOG

IDEAL DAY

March 20th — With the exception of a snow droze about 9 a.m., the day was another ideal sealers' day. Ship started at 5 a.m. to place the men on the ice, but found seals very scarce. Put out some men. Started picking up pans. *Bonaventure* and *Eagle* came into the patch during the past night. During the evening the *Sagona* also steamed in from the N.W.

The *Bloodhound*, *Florizel* and *Fogota* are also in the patch inside. The *Stephano*, *Beothic* and *Bellaventure* are in sight picking up pans. Too far off to know what they are doing except by wireless which at this juncture is anything but reliable. Belle Isle reports that sixty miles of seals passed along during the month. There must be a large patch of seals to the South East.

The ice is broken up owing to being forced on Belle Isle. That makes it hard for panning and has scattered the number of seals somewhat. Fully ten per cent of the young seals have escaped as a few here and there on a pan are not worth stopping to take.

Weighed several pelts today. They average fifty-five pounds; some weighed seventy-three, one only fifty. The pelts are in the primest condition. Weighed carcasses which average twenty-five pounds for young.

SPLENDID SIGHT

Did not go on ice today; no good chance. Splendid sight to see foredeck piled with five thousand seals. All in this patch were cut up. Expect to finish taking on board tonight and be off to the S.E. in search of another patch without delay.

We will have about twelve thousand out of this patch which do not exceed fifty thousand, the *Stephano*, *Beothic* and *Bellaventure* have probably taken ten thousand each; the other ships about eight thousand.

The Captain is a very cool man. Absolutely proof against excitement. Very little shouting. The old sealer, Skipper Peter Gaulton, is without doubt a sealing expert. What he doesn't know about seals and their habits and the handling of a ship in the seals and out very few can teach him.

The Captain's son Pearcey is second in command and is a chip from the old block in every respect. He says little but takes in the whole situation at a glance.

The crew are delighted. Every man carries a smile, and there is nothing but good said about the food.

JEWEL OF A COOK

The cook—Samuel Tiller—is indeed a jewel so far as his duties go, and the cook's duties are performed like clock work. Sammy is constantly on the alert, and his assistants are all performing their parts creditably.

The Doctor has developed into an expert winch manipulator and all the men say he is the only Doctor gentleman they ever sailed with.

If any one attempt to take over the work of driving the winch he is received with a head shake from the Doctor which is good as saying: "No thank you, I am boss of this machine."

Amid the bustle and clutter of a sealing steamer worked a well-ordered crew. Much like a military unit, the men were divided by rank and everyone had a role to play. *The Rooms Provincial Archives Division, VA 137-50*

There was a hierarchy among the sealers. The ship's master reigned at the top and with absolute authority. Immediately below him was the second hand—a veteran sealer who might also be called the first mate or ice mate. Sometimes the second hand left the ship to hunt seals, but he typically remained on board the steamer with the captain.

Next were the master watches, usually about four per vessel. They commanded up to 50 or more men and received orders directly from the captain and second hand. On the ice, the master watch divided his men into smaller groups and put an experienced sealer in charge of each unit (or ice party). This man was known as an ice master—a name also given to the vessel's captain.

An ice master's authority ended when he boarded the vessel, where another crewmember, known as the stow boss or deck router, was second in command to the master watch. He directed various shipboard activities, such as the stowing of pelts or coal. If a master watch died or became badly injured, the deck router took his place.

Life Aboard Ship

A sealing steamer was home to between 100 and 300 men for several weeks at a time. Yet life aboard ship was only marginally more comfortable than it was on the floes. The sealers lived in a dirty and cramped area between decks sometimes known as the dungeon. They slept on rough wooden planks and had to bring their own bedding, usually bags filled with wood shavings. There were rarely enough bunks to go around, so most men had to share. They slept and worked in the same unwashed clothing. Bathing was impossible. Before too long, the filth and stink of blood (seal and human), sweat, seal fat, coal dust, tobacco, and wet dirty clothing filled the makeshift living quarters. If the hunt was good, the seal pelts spilled into the dungeon and the men slept on these. To say that they roughed it is an understatement.

Not everyone who went to the floes took part in the hunt. Engineers, oilers, coal trimmers, and firemen sweated in the engine room below, while a small team of sailors manned the decks above. A boatswain cared for gaffs, ropes, and other equipment and saw to it that the sealers were properly outfitted before they jumped overboard. Cooks were on every vessel, and doctors on many. Some captains also brought along their own steward.

If a vessel had telegraph equipment, it also carried a wireless operator—known as the Marconi man. The *Florizel* became the first sealing steamer to use this technology in 1909, and others soon followed suit. The public devoured daily updates printed in local newspapers and posted in telegraph offices, while merchants kept close tabs on their investments at the floes. Captains who worked for the same firms wired each other directions to the best hunting grounds—using secret codes to conceal such sensitive information.

This technology brought a small degree of safety to a dangerous industry. Captains could alert each other of bad weather and ice conditions, or ask for help if their men got into trouble. But the equipment was expensive and not all merchant firms thought it would add to their earnings. The government finally made wireless equipment mandatory in 1916, after an already angry public learned that if the *Newfoundland* had been carrying wireless equipment in 1914, the disaster would have likely been averted.

“It wasn't very comfortable in those old bunks. Half of the fellows didn't have bunks. Only a hard board or something and a blanket thrown down there. No pillow. A clothes bag to carry your clothes in for a pillow. You'd look out there in the gloom and in the dark of the hold. If she was rolling the old lanterns would swing back and forth.... There was nothing cozy about it, not a thing in the world. Only a bad smell that would make you seasick if you wasn't used to going to sea.”

—Cecil Mouland, *Newfoundland* survivor

ASCD, Coll. 115 16.04.033

NOTHING BUT RISK AND PERIL

MR. COAKER'S LOG

March 21st — Wind N.W. by N., strong, with snow most of the day. Frosty and very unpleasant. See no distance. Took about five hundred seals in small patches. Working out to S.E. Ice heavy. Passed *Bonaventure* and *Bloodhound*. Ships on inside taking on board panned seals. Our ship endeavouring to get away to S.E. as a large patch of seals still remain untouched and that patch must be in the South East.

Mosie Waterman met with slight accident yesterday, one of the hatch planks fell and struck his toe, apparently breaking it, but Mosie's tongue is still as lively as ever. He will be about in a day or two if he will remain still and not use his foot.

March 22nd — *Bonaventure* reports man dead—Henry Pridham, of Petty Harbour, having died from injuries sustained by falling though the after hatch on the night of the 20th and died early this morning. The *Bonaventure* has no doctor. Our doctor went on board at noon today. The *Bonaventure* having come up to us, *Bonaventure* and *Nascopie* in company all day. Did not steam much. At night seven ships in sight.

Men had divine service on board three times today, with much singing of hymns. Rosary also said by R.C. friends. Being Sunday the cooks had extra work to prepare the Sunday food for the crew. All expressed themselves as being well satisfied with the food on Mondays as well as Sundays. The cooks work night and day with sweat rolling off them. To cook the food now provided by law the cooks must keep constantly to work. Only once so far this voyage have the cooks done any other work. When all the men are on the ice and the cooks are willing to handle seals, one or two may be spared for an hour or two, but only once have I seen a cook handling seals.

TRUE TO SPIRIT

The captain is true to the spirit of the law in reference to cooks; he abstained from ordering them to handle seals, and what was done was the voluntary act of a subordinate cook with the consent of the chief.

The sealers on the *Nascopie* absolutely refused to consent to allow the cooks to handle seals. I hope this matter of taking the cooks from their proper duties to handle seals is now about fixed. I don't think the men on any ship will in future be willing to have the cooking neglected in order to allow two or three cooks to handle seals. It will not be tolerated in future, and what will be lost by keeping the cooks at their own work will not amount to much.

FAITHFULLY PERFORMED

Captain Barbour has faithfully performed his part in carrying out the sealing regulations. The owners have done their part, for the food was placed on board of this ship. The chief cook has done his part nobly. The greatest responsibility rests upon the chief cook, for he can make things go right if he feels so inclined. The assistant cooks have all done their parts well. The steward has also done his part well.

It will be difficult to have all the crews treated alike, unless there is one man placed on each ship by law, whose duty it will be to see that the regulations are observed, and to make immediate complaint where there is any negligence and failing improvement immediately after a complaint is lodged with the captain, notice should at once be given on a suit for breach of the regulations. After two or three years such an official could be dispensed with, as the men would by then recognize their full rights and what the regulations called for, and would see them enforced.

TWELVE MEN ASTRAY

Beothic had 12 men astray on the ice until 11p.m. When found they had prepared an ice house made from clumpers, and were enjoying a fire of seal carcasses and pelts. A larger number of the *Beothic*'s crew who were astray boarded the *Stephano* earlier in the evening.

March 22 brought with it the first fatality of the 1914 seal hunt. Two nights earlier (some reports say three), Henry Pridham climbed out of the dungeon and onto the *Bonaventure*'s main deck. By then, a slimy film of seal blood, grease, ice, and slush encased the vessel. Pridham slipped and fell through a hatch into the hold below, smashing his head against the edge of a coal tub. He sank into unconsciousness, but no one considered bringing him home for treatment, not while there were seals to kill. Pridham died on March 22. His wife and four children had to wait until April 7 for the *Bonaventure* to return to St. John's.

Death, disease, and injury stalked every sealer at the icefields. Drowning and freezing to death were the most obvious threats. Broken bones were another. If a sealer slipped near his vessel, he could get pinned between its hull and the ice. The pressure could easily crush his legs and even kill him. The frequent use of gunpowder to blast jammed ships free of tight ice brought with it other dangers. The men had to move fast to avoid the explosion and then dodge the many shards of ice it sent flying. The engine room claimed its fatalities too, first in 1874 when the *Tigress*'s boilers exploded and scalded 21 men to death.

Disease was another problem. The sealing steamers, filthy and overcrowded, were home to frequent bouts of dysentery. Smallpox and measles had broken out on occasion too. One of the most notorious diseases, and unique to pinniped (fin-footed mammals) hunters, was known as seal finger. This painful infection was transmitted from a seal pelt to a cut or abrasion on the sealer's hand. A victim's finger became swollen and excruciat-

Sealers risked injury, sickness, and even death to work at the floes.
ASCD, Coll. 203 7.01.044

The Evening Herald, St. John's

Out Of The Jaws Of Death

Perils and Tragedies of

The Sealing Industry

Thrilling Tales Of The Hazards That Attend the Reaping Of the Harvest of The Floes.

ingly painful for a few weeks before healing in a permanently crooked position. The finger was useless for fishing and most other work, so many sealers had it amputated, until doctors learned they could treat the infection with antibiotics.

There was also ice blindness, accompanied by intense pain and temporarily reduced vision. Bright sunlight bounced off the vast white floes and scorched an unprotected eye's cornea. The victim felt like his eyelids had turned to sandpaper. After a day or two, the pain disappeared and normal sight returned. Sealers wore goggles or smeared seal blood around their eyes to protect against this torment.

The Newfoundland government did not pass legislation making doctors (or at the very least pharmacists) mandatory on sealing vessels—but only on those carrying more than 150 sealers—until 1916.

THE THREE "VENTURES," NEW TYPE SEALING STEAMERS, NEWFOUN

Inquest About Sealer's Death.

The magisterial enquiry into the death of sealer Pridham terminated before Judge Knight at one o'clock to-day, when the last witness was examined. Evidence was given that no light near the hatch of the S.S. Bonaventure and the deceased in passing along the deck of the ship one evening fell into the hold and was so seriously hurt that death followed. It is said there will be an action taken against the owners of the ship.

Henry Pridham's death aboard the *Bonaventure* (right) was the first fatality of the 1914 hunt. *MHA, PF-001.1-M03a; Evening Telegram, May 7, 1914*

The sealers risked their lives and suffered weeks of severe privation, but the most they ever got in return was a small sum of cash—barely enough to make ends meet. Why did so many men return to the ice year after year?

Some went for the adventure. The seal hunt had a storied past that was celebrated in songs and the press. But dreams of adventure did not underpin the hunt. It was real-life poverty that chased most sealers onto the ice.

Newfoundland offered its outport residents little in the way of employment and social services. The sealers were desperately and inescapably poor. They worked in the cod fishery, but even that centuries-old industry could not put food on the table all year. If they went to the floes, and if the hunting was good, the men could return to their families with a small share of the profits. It was nothing compared to what the merchants and captains earned, but to a fisher living in a land ruled by merchant credit, any quantity of cash was a rare luxury.

MHA, PF-001.p034

THE EVENING TELEGRAM, ST. JOHN'S, NEWFOUNDLAND, MAY 7, 1914—6

The Holloway Studio, Limited.

Sealers Notice !

As notice has been given by the Board of Health that all persons going to the Seal Fishery the coming Spring must have been vaccinated Recently, no person will be signed for the "NASCOPIE," "BEOTHIC," "NEPTUNE," "DIANA" and "ERIK" unless they can produce certificate of vaccination.

JOB BROS. & CO., LTD.

Sealers Notice !

It will be necessary for those who have procured berths in "ERNA," "BLOODHOUND" and "SOUTHERN CROSS," to produce, before signing articles, a certificate certifying that they have been vaccinated within the past seven years.

BAINE, JOHNSTON & CO

To prevent the spread of disease, sealers had to be vaccinated before boarding a steamer. *Evening Telegram, January 12, 1912*

THE ICE CAPTAINS

The ice captains in 1902. Back row (left to right): Isaac Mercer, D. Blandford, Job Kean, Alf Barbour, Isaac Mercer Jr., and George Barbour. Front row: Chas Dawe, George Hann, A. Kean, H.D. Reid, Arthur Jackman, and Sam Blandford. *MHA, PF-315.107*

The ice captains loomed large in Newfoundland. Powerful, fearsome, and brave, their names rang out all over the island, and so did wild tales of their exploits. Take Captain Arthur Jackman of Renews ("the Old Scorcher")—he mangled his finger at the floes one year but didn't even lose a beat, just called for an axe and chopped it clean off, standing right there on the deck of his vessel. "I don't care who was the best man before I come," he'd growl. "I'm the best one now."

All the ice captains had that same attitude, that same swagger. Spring

MR. COAKER'S LOG

March 23rd — Crew out at 2 a.m. pelting seals. Ice very tight and heavy: about the tightest experienced since leaving St. John's. Our position is about thirty miles South East of Belle Isle. The *Bellaventure* and *Bonaventure* in company, while the *Florizel* and *Fogota* lay about 5 miles to the N.W. The *Beothic* and a larger steamer supposed to be the *Stephano* lay about 10 miles East of us. Bay clear and no wind. Impossible to search for seals as ice too tight and heavy. So far as we can judge about 90,000 seals taken to date. All of these were taken between Belle Isle and Groais Island. Took about 900 seals today. Slight swell on which in latter part of the day permitted the ships to get around.

BEST FOR VOYAGE

Seals taken today best for the voyage. Weighed several that tipped the scales at 70 pounds. Average 60 or five pounds better than two days ago.

Young taking to the water, coats becoming spotted. Mothers left the young, they will now decrease in weight. Very few old seals now seen on the ice or in the water. *Stephano* panned a few today to east of us. *Stephano* had four men astray during the early part of the night.

We have today passed through much of the whelping ice from which the first seals were taken. The whelping ice has drifted about 50 miles during the last eight days—or about six miles in 24 hours.

DISPUTE AS TO QUANTITY

A dispute arose in the fore hold regarding the quantity of seals brought in since 1900 by Captains George Barbour and Ab. Kean. Dr. Bunting sought *Chafe's Sealing Guide* which proved that during the last 13 years—1900 to 1913—Captain George Barbour brought in 3,142 seals more than Captain Kean. The figures being:

Barbour 365,994
Kean 362,852

This settled the dispute and a pound of F.P.U. tobacco changed hands.

Another dispute arose as to how many springs have passed since Capt. Wm. Barbour brought in two loads the one spring in the *Diana*, and what amount the men made. Reference was again made to *Chafe's Guide*, when it was shown that Capt. Wm. Barbour made his notable trips 23 springs ago, and his men shared $182.30.

Mosie Waterman, of Fair Island, in this case won the forfeit. It turned out that Mosie was a stowaway on the *Diana* that spring and behaved so well that the crew gave him a full share. Consequently it surprised none to find that Mosie remembered the year so well.

ALMOST A JINK

In going over Chafe's book to confirm the doctor's figures, I noticed that Capt. Ab. Kean almost made a jink of it in 1905, when his voyage numbered 4,553, and his men made the small bill of $13.97. Capt. Geo. Barbour's worse year during the period referred to, was 1904, when he brought in 12,874, his men sharing $34.86. The value of seals brought in by Capt. George Barbour in 14 springs, exceed by $15,000 the value of seals brought in by Capt. Ab. Kean during the same period.

after spring, they steamed out, hungering not only for pelts and profits but also for glory. They demanded absolute obedience from their crews.

In the era of sail, almost any hardworking and ambitious sealer could realistically expect to move his way up the ladder and one day command his own vessel. But that was when the fleet consisted of hundreds of schooners, built and owned in dozens of outport communities. Steam changed everything. By 1914, only several dozen steamers, and captains, prosecuted the seal hunt. Commanding a steamer required special skills. Captains began to apprentice their sons and nephews, and an aristocracy soon emerged within the industry, dominated by a few prominent sealing families: the Keans, the Bartletts, the Winsors, or the Blandfords.

But a captaincy was not entirely a birthright. If an ice master did not perform at the floes, the merchant firm that employed him could easily find a replacement. Many careers ended after only one or two trips north. The trick was not just in locating the big herds but also in reaching them before anyone else did—or better yet, without anyone else noticing. There were other, less honest, tricks too, and not all captains were above stealing a rival's unguarded pan of pelts. An ice master's worth, after all, was measured in the number of seals he brought home. Nothing else mattered.

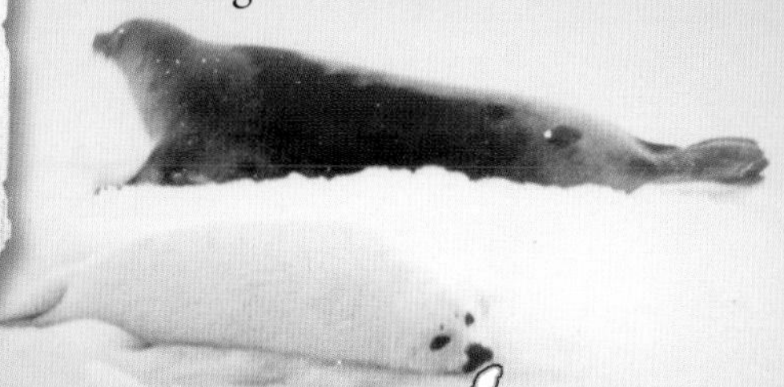

Abram Kean, before 1917. *The Rooms Provincial ArchivesDivision, A 23-83*

Abram Kean:
The Admiral of the Fleet

Known as the Admiral (or Commodore) of the Fleet, Abram Kean has been called the most successful and famous sealing captain of all time. Born in 1855 to a fishing family at Flowers Island, Bonavista Bay, he became a fisher at 13, a sealer at 17, and a master watch at 20. He spent these early years aboard his brother's schooner, the *Peerless*, but worked hard to make the transition from sail to steam. In 1884, he secured a spot aboard the sealing steamer *Ranger*, under Captain Joe Barbour. Five years later, he was captain of the SS *Wolf* and brought home the second-largest catch of the season. Kean carved out a reputation as a gifted, but ruthless, ice captain. He became a controversial figure in the 1898 *Greenland* disaster, after he was accused of stealing that vessel's pans of pelts (a claim that was never proved). If the *Greenland*'s men did not have to make up their losses, some said, they would not have been out hunting in bad weather. Public opinion would later hold Kean morally responsible for the 1914 *Newfoundland* disaster too. But his successes outshone his notoriety. Kean had an unparalleled ability to locate the herds, and sealers would do almost anything for a berth on his vessel. In 1934, he won widespread praise (and an appointment to the Order of the British Empire) for bringing home his one-millionth seal pelt. He also excelled in other areas. Kean was twice elected to the Newfoundland House of Assembly (in 1885 and 1897) and in 1898 became the minister of the newly created Department of Marine and Fisheries. He retired from the seal hunt in 1936, and died on May 18, 1945.

The Spoils of the Hunt

MR. COAKER'S LOG

March 24th — Thick most of the day. Took about 300 seals. Ship moving all day, but found no new patch. Most of the steamers in our vicinity. Reports received from them show that we have so far done as well as most of them.

FINE LOT OF SKINS

Adventure has picked up a fine lot of seals this week, probably done the best work of the fleet since Monday. We cut through 21 miles of ice surrounding the ice from which the seals secured were taken. We burnt down for the night near the *Stephano*. We have about 13,000 stowed to date. Our ship calls 21 seals 20 in counting, the reason advanced for so doing is, to be sure not to hail for more than is on board. The system of counting is very reliable.

All the seals taken during the day are placed on deck. When the work on ice for the day is over, the watches in turn stow the seals below. They are thrown into a chute which direct them below, and each seal is counted one by one. Every man crying out the number in rotation.

Each 21 seals are tallied by the master watch on a board. The tally is made by cutting a notch on the edge of the board. Each notch means 20 seals.

The landsmen in future in reckoning the seals reported as on board will add 5 per cent if he wishes to find out the exact number on board the *Nascopie*.

Weighed several seal pelts, averaged 60 lbs. Weighed one round white coat, weight 85 lbs, found carcass 15 lbs, blood about 8 lbs.

Steamers unload their catch at the Job Brothers premises in St. John's harbour, ca. 1905. *MHA, PF-315.090*

Everyone at the floes wanted the same thing: to be on the vessel that brought home the most pelts. The rewards for doing so were enormous: money, prestige, and, if the catch was large enough, a permanent place in the folklore of the hunt. The icefields were recruiting grounds for Newfoundland's heroes and legends.

Money was by far the biggest reward for the sealers. They worked for a small share of their vessel's catch, so the more pelts they brought home, the more cash they made. The average pay between 1900 and 1914 was $39.53 per sealer, but the men stood to earn more if their vessel reached a big patch of seals before the rest of the fleet. Everyone remembered 1910, when Abram Kean's men earned $148.36 each.

Crews sometimes returned home empty-handed, sabotaged by bad weather, a jammed vessel, or an inexperienced captain. Worse, at the end of the hunt they could owe money. Merchant firms charged the sealers between $9 and $15 for their "crop"—supplies and equipment the men bought on credit (and at greatly inflated prices) before leaving port, such as boots and goggles.

The captains were also in it for the money, and they took home a much larger share of the catch than the sealers. In 1910, Abram Kean earned $3,632 for about a month's work—25 times more than what his men earned and more than double the annual salary of the General Hospital's chief resident physician. A good sealing captain could

Below: Men waiting for a berth on a sealing vessel, ca. 1905. *MHA, PF-316.027*

Finding a Berth

The competition that marked the seal hunt began long before the vessels reached the icefields. Every winter, thousands of outport men vied with each other to secure a berth aboard a sealing steamer. Sometimes the vessels came to the outports to recruit crew, and sometimes the merchants gave tickets to local politicians and clergy to distribute as they saw fit. But many men also had to visit St. John's "on spec" to apply to the merchant firms for a berth. They arrived by rail and they arrived by foot. It was not uncommon for men to walk 50 miles or more in the hopes of securing a ticket to the ice floes. But the number of applicants far exceeded the number of berths and many men returned home empty-handed.

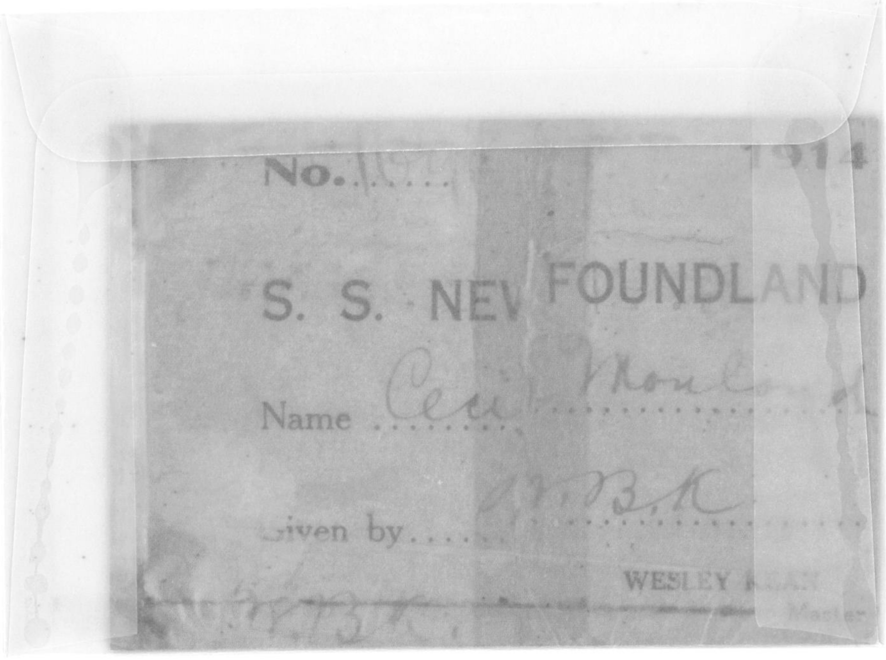
No. ... 1914

S. S. NEWFOUNDLAND

Name ...

Given by ...

WESLEY

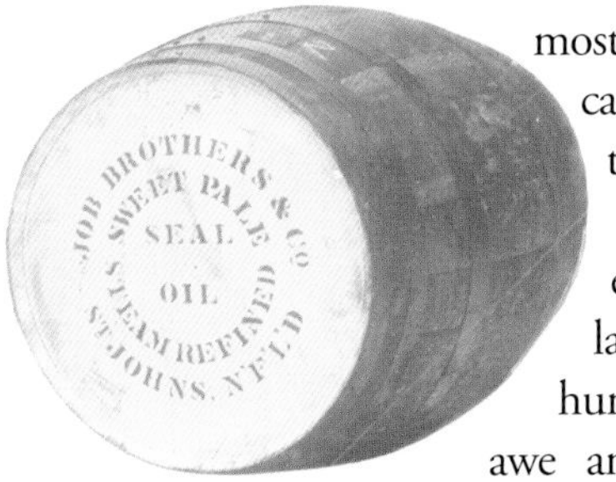

become fabulously wealthy. But most were not content with cash alone. They wanted the glory too.

More than anyone else, the captains populated the folklore of the hunt. Their names inspired awe and respect, and some were remembered for generations. Each spring, they competed fiercely to bring home the most pelts and win the prestigious title of high liner. Whoever succeeded would be paid in money and respect, and perhaps even earn a permanent place in Newfoundland history. Fame and wealth also gave them power—more than one captain was elected to political office or established his own merchant firm.

Seal oil was a valuable commodity.
MHA, PF315.140

Hoisting pelts onto the deck of the *Nascopie*, where they will cool before being stowed below, ca. 1930.
MHA, PF-118.022

Leisure Time

MR. COAKER'S LOG

March 25th — Fine day. Nine steamers in sight all day. Passed *Stephano* and *Bonaventure*. Took about 1,000 during the day. Steamed to S. East and again to West. Must have covered 100 miles during the day in search of a new patch. Steamed most of the night. Report from the two fleets, front and gulf, received. Glad to find Gulf ships did so well.

GRAMOPHONE CONCERT

Had gramophone concert in ball room for crew between 8 and 9 p.m., which helped the leisure hour to pass pleasantly. Skipper James Harris, of Harbour Grace, elected mock king of the common sealers. His duty is to govern the crew and to enforce sealers' sea laws. The king is aided by a judge, sheriff, and two constables. Each offender is reported to the court by the king and the court, hears all cases and where necessary submits the case to a jury. The prisoner and king is represented by a lawyer. The two lawyers selected being Chief Engineer Leddingham and Dr. Bunting. The writer being selected for judge.

March 26th — Splendid day. Fine, warm and clear. Steamed into a small patch of seals about 8 a.m. The *Beothic* in company. Many of the seals dipping. A number able to handle themselves in the water very well. Ice open. In small pans. Very difficult to get about on ice. *Beothic* cut us off about noon and by so doing took quite a number of seals from our men. Spoke to several of *Beothic*'s men. They hail for 22,000, with seven pans out. Reported with two blades of propellor broken. *Beothic* has been in the seals continuously from the start.

We took 2,500 seals today, and have about 17,000 seals on board. Had men on the ice until after darkness set in. The day was the best in point of weather experienced since leaving port. The sun's rays warm as the day was calm throughout.

Sealers with the steamer *Beothic* take a break during the 1911 seal hunt.
The Rooms Provincial Archives Division, VA 44-40

There was little opportunity for rest or play when the men were "in the fat," but they did sometimes have spare time. This might be when the steamer was prowling the icefields for seals or when bad weather kept everyone trapped inside. There could also be a period of inactivity on the ice, when the day's hunting was over and the men still had to wait for their vessel to pick them up.

Cards and checkers were popular pastimes aboard the ship, but the men also invented games using the tools at hand. One was a kind of ring toss using bits of rope tied in small circles and two knives driven into the deck a few feet apart from each other. Woodcarving was another popular activity and required nothing more than a broken gaff, the sealer's knife, and his imagination.

Imagination was in no short supply among the men, who were more than capable of entertaining each other by inventing role-playing games like the mock court case described by Coaker in his journal. The sealers also loved to sing songs, recite poems, and tell stories. Sea shanties and love ballads were popular, and so were pirate legends, fishing yarns, and tales of banshees, ghosts, and the supernatural. But it was the seal hunt itself that produced the most compelling subject matter.

Some of the most popular songs and stories glorified the hunt's past. There was a time, they said, when sealers were so strong that they didn't even have to climb over the side of a vessel to get back on board—they

COME ALL YE JOLLY ICE-HUNTERS

This song was written in 1833. It is about the oldest song of a sealing nature now in existence, and has "brought down the house" in the for'castle of many a sealer in the days of the Square Riggers.

Come all ye jolly ice-hunters and listen to my song
I hope I won't offend you, I don't mean to keep you long.
'Tis concerning an ice-hunter, from Tilton Harbour sailed away.
On the fourteenth day of March, eighteen hundred and thirty-three.

William Burke was our commander, the "Daniel O'Connell" was our good ship's name.
We had twenty-eight as smart a lads as ever crossed the main;
As off with flying colors to the northward we did steer,
So mark what followed after, to you I will declare.

'Twas on the fourth of April, right well I mind the day;
About four o'clock in the evening our towline gave away;
The wind came from the northwest and bitterly did blow,
Our captain cries, "Stand by, my b'ys, out of the ice we'll have to go.

"Stand by your topsail halliards; stand by to let them go,
Be quick, I say, make no delay, your topsail clear also";
He watched his opportunity and soon he had her free,
Saying, God bless the "Brave O'Connell" see how she stems the sea.

At six o'clock next morning we were a dreadful wreck,
Our topmast went overboard about three feet from the deck;
In this perilous condition for two long days we lay,
So we left her to God's mercy, and to the raging sea.

We could not keep a light below, the seas ran mountains high,
And expecting every minute that we were doomed to die;
At eight o'clock next morning all hands were called on deck,
Some to rig up jury masts, and more to clear the wreck.

Now a few days after, assistance was at hand,
At six o'clock in the morning, the watch espied the land;
So now, thanks unto Providence, we're safe on shore at last,
We'll drink to one another and drown sorrow in the glass.

From *Old Time Songs and Poetry of Newfoundland*, 1927, by Gerald S. Doyle.
Reproduced with permission from the Doyle Family

The Rooms Provincial Archives Division, VA 44-29

just jumped over the rail in a single mighty bound, towing their pelts behind them. Then there was the amazing spring of 1872, when Captain Azariah Munden was so successful in finding the big herds that he had to stuff seals into every nook and cranny of his vessel and still tow 600 more behind him. The ship rode so low that the men could just reach over its side and dip their hands in the water.

There were also tragedies, which needed no embellishment. The *Greenland* disaster, for example, or the sinking of the *Mastiff* in 1898, which left all of its crew stranded on the ice, scantily clad and in the middle of a terrible storm, before rescue arrived the next day. Every sealer hoped that if his name did one day appear in a song or story, it would not be a sad one.

Other Kinds of Sealers

MR. COAKER'S LOG

March 27th — Came across few seals pelted by landsmen, weight of pelts 30 lbs. Found a knife and piece of unravelled rope on pan, also an old harp seal. The ice must have cut Cape Bauld shore. We are now 60 miles N.N.E. of Funk Island. Weather thick, which has caused young seals to take to the water. Very little will be done in capturing them, except we get fine sunny days.

SPOKE TO *FOGOTA*

Took about 800 seals today. Spoke to *Fogota* at nightfall. She reports for 2,000. *Beothic*, *Eagle*, *Bonaventure* in our vicinity. James Davis, of Wesleyville, dislocated arm by a tumble over pinnacle. Doctor soon set it, as the accident happened near the ship. The poor chap lost one half of dislocated arm some years ago caused by the explosion of a gun.

Our position now about 50 miles N.E. of Funk Island. Passed a few of the *Beothic*'s missing pans, which were subsequently picked up by the *Beothic*.

Fogota spent the night alongside of us. Some of her crew complained loudly about the grub supplied and non-compliance with the sealing law.

They reported shortage in sugar, beans, potatoes. No fresh beef or brewse had been supplied as per regulations. One of the favoured few on her swallowed all the whisky he could get on board of our ship, and begged all the tobacco obtainable. He has a long winded tongue and before reaching his own ship was privileged to a "ducking" in the briny icy waters. We wished them good luck and much success with the old [seals] later on.

Landsmen hunted seals on foot and in small open boats. This man's eight seal carcasses could help support a family through the long winter. *The Rooms Provincial Archives Division, VA 118-33.8*

Not everyone who hunted seals in Newfoundland and Labrador joined the steamer industry. Families who lived in coastal Labrador and the island's northern bays could operate from a land base. Winds and tides usually brought the whelping ice so close to their coasts that sealers could row to the herds in small open boats. If they were lucky, the ice came right up to the shore and they could just walk out to the seals and drag back some pelts. Men, women, and even children hunted seals this way. They were known as landsmen.

The landsmen fishery was much smaller than the vessel-based hunt, but it was also much older. It dates back to the early 1700s when European migratory fishing crews overwintered in northeast Newfoundland. They noticed that harp seals appeared in coastal waters almost every winter and spring, and they began to hunt the mammal for its meat, oil, and pelt. The seal hunt complemented the summer cod fishery and made Newfoundland's northeast coast an attractive place for settlement. The area was soon home to the island's most famous sealing centres in Bonavista and Notre Dame bays.

The landsmen fishery was eventually eclipsed by the vessel-based hunt, but it remained a vital part of the seasonal round in northeast Newfoundland and coastal Labrador. Without it, many families would not have survived.

Meat and money from the seal hunt supplemented other activities—fishing in the summer, hunting in the fall, woodcutting in the winter, and gardening in the spring and summer. The landsmen had to rely on weather and waves to bring the seals to them, unlike the steamer crews, who tracked down the herds year after year in increasingly powerful vessels.

Conflict occasionally erupted between these two kinds of sealers. Some ice captains considered the landsmen a nuisance and complained that they stole their pans of pelts. Similarly, some landsmen accused the vessel-based hunt of reducing the herds to dangerously low levels. This was indeed the case by 1914, when the harp seals showed signs of depletion.

Pack ice often drifted close to Newfoundland's northern shore, allowing communities like St. Anthony (top) and Twillingate to take part in the landsmen fishery.
MHA, PF-325.056 (top) and PF-035.009 (bottom)

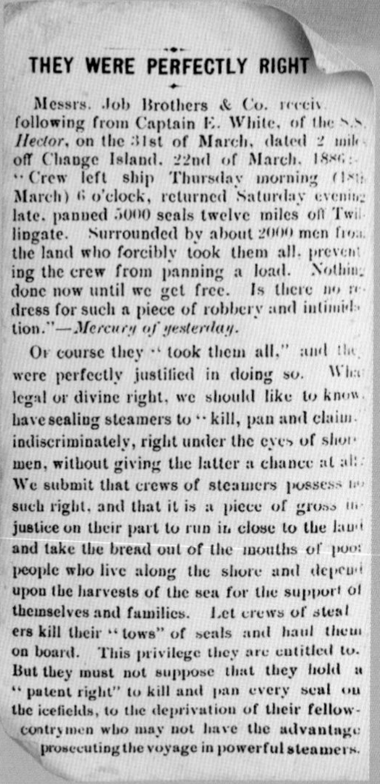

THEY WERE PERFECTLY RIGHT

Messrs. Job Brothers & Co. receiv[illegible] following from Captain E. White, of the S.S. *Hector*, on the 31st of March, dated 2 mil[illegible] off Change Island, 22nd of March, 1886:—"Crew left ship Thursday morning (18th March) 6 o'clock, returned Saturday evening late, panned 5000 seals twelve miles off Twillingate. Surrounded by about 2000 men from the land who forcibly took them all, preventing the crew from panning a load. Nothing done now until we get free. Is there no redress for such a piece of robbery and intimidation."—*Mercury of yesterday.*

Of course they "took them all," and the[illegible] were perfectly justified in doing so. Wha[illegible] legal or divine right, we should like to know, have sealing steamers to "kill, pan and claim" indiscriminately, right under the eyes of shoremen, without giving the latter a chance at all? We submit that crews of steamers possess no such right, and that it is a piece of gross injustice on their part to run in close to the land and take the bread out of the mouths of poor people who live along the shore and depend upon the harvests of the sea for the support of themselves and families. Let crews of steamers kill their "tows" of seals and haul them on board. This privilege they are entitled to. But they must not suppose that they hold a "patent right" to kill and pan every seal on the icefields, to the deprivation of their fellow-contrymen who may not have the advantage [illegible] prosecuting the voyage in powerful steamers.

This anonymous letter to the editor of the *Evening Telegram* shows the tensions that existed between the vessel-based seal hunt and the landsmen (called "shoremen" here).
Evening Telegram, April 1, 1886

Aboriginal Seal Hunters

For as long as there have been people in Newfoundland and Labrador, there has been a seal hunt. Prehistoric groups such as the Thule, Maritime Archaic, and Little Passage people prized seals for their meat, oil, skin, and fur. The same is true of their ancestors—the Innu and Inuit in Labrador and the Beothuk on the island. The Mi'kmaq also hunted seals in the Gulf of St. Lawrence.

With their sharp blades of ivory, bone, or stone, toggling harpoons were common and effective weapons in the seal hunt. Hunters caught seals on land, through sea ice, and from boats—small one-person vessels, such as a kayak, or larger vessels able to hold a dozen or more people.

Aboriginal groups used all parts of a seal: they ate the meat, drank the blood, burned the oil, and used the bones to manufacture weapons, tools, ornaments, and other utensils. Sealskin was waterproof and provided excellent material for boots, coats, mittens, and other clothing, and a good covering for shelters and boats.

Innu seal hunters in the Gulf of St. Lawrence.
Drawn by W.G.R. Hind, chromolithographed by Hanhard

In the Pantry

MR. COAKER'S LOG

March 28th —Took an S.E. course at daybreak, accompanied by the *Adventure*, and steamed South of the Funks in search of a new patch, but saw nothing in the shape of seals. Ice much scattered and broken. Weather thick, wind blowing a gale from the N.W. Took no seals. *Adventure* kept close to us all day and both ships burnt down at nightfall within hailing distance of each other.

Adventure's crew bitterly complained concerning negligence of chief cook in not providing meals according to the sealing laws. Fresh beef was served once, having been boiled instead of roasted. Brewse only served twice to date. No breakfast being cooked on Sunday, as all cooks but one lay in bunk until 7:30 a.m. and the chief cook loudly proclaimed that he would cook breakfast for no one. He must be noted and prevented from sailing again as a cook.

COOKS OBJECT

Adventure's men say Capt. Kean anxious to have meals served according to rules, but cooks refuse to do so. It will be necessary to amend sealing law and provide for the placing of an official on board of each ship to see that regulations are observed and in case of default to institute action against cooks, master and owner. Cooks will also have to be paid a bonus by the owners in addition to a share of the voyage, as their duties continually demand all their time and they work 18 hours every day. They probably put in three times as much time on duty as any of the men in the underdeck. A bonus of $20 should be paid to each assistant cook and baker, and $30 to the chief cook, then the chief cook will be in a position to demand the close attention of the assistants, which they don't feel like doing under the present circumstances.

MUST BE ALIKE

Every ship must supply meals alike and all sealers must be accorded similar food, and until such conditions are accomplished, there must be no "let up" on behalf of the F.P.U. and toilers of the deep.

The experience afforded me as a result of this voyage to the icefields, will, I trust, result beneficially for those who tread the frozen pans.

Captain George Barbour has continually interested himself in the matter of the food of his crew since leaving port, and makes it his duty to visit the cooks' quarters regularly and consult with the chief cook in order to see that the regulations are respected and observed on board the *Nascopie*.

STEAMED ALL DAY

March 29th — Ship steaming all day. No seals. *Adventure* and *Beothic* in company. Held sacred gramophone concert in hold for crew. Methodist service held in afternoon and night by Ariel Burt, of Old Perlican, who has led service at the seal fishery under Captain Barbour's command for eight years. I attended evening service. Splendid order prevailed throughout the ship during service. The singing was excellent. The strong voices of 100 men singing some of the grand old hymns was something to be long remembered.

The only black spot I noticed was the action of one Henry Lockyer, of Bay de Verde, who outraged the feelings of all who attended the service by chewing tobacco. The indecency of such an action did not seem to disturb him, as he afterwards gloated over the incident when it was brought to his notice by one of those who attended.

AWAY TO THE NORTH

The ship steamed over a large distance during the day and apparently Captain Barbour decided there was no seals South as he headed for the North in the afternoon. Most of the men had washed, shaved, and were dressed in holiday attire.

The *Beothic* reports for 25,000 [pelts] and hopes to reach St. John's by Wednesday.

The galley of a wooden sealing steamer, likely the *Vanguard*, in 1902. With more than 100 men to feed, the cook's job was never done—and he didn't get a day off on Sundays like the sealers did. *Photo by William Howe Greene*

A sealer's diet lacked variety. Hard bread and black tea were the staples, occasionally and inconsistently supplemented by fish and brewis, salt pork, duff, or the odd vegetable. Coaker wanted to change that. Shortly before boarding the *Nascopie,* he passed a sealing bill in the Newfoundland House of Assembly which was aimed in part at forcing merchant firms to provide the sealers with better food.

The bill stipulated that the sealers be given soft bread, salt beef or pork, potatoes, and duff three times a week. Breakfasts would alternate between beans and fish and brewis. On Saturdays, there would be soup made with turnips, onions, and potatoes. Fresh, or at the very least canned, beef would be served once a week. As usual, there would be as much hard bread, black tea, molasses, and butter (or, failing that, raw salted fatback) as the men could consume.

Job Brothers made sure that the *Nascopie* followed the new rules during the 1914 seal hunt, but many other merchant firms ignored them. On March 28, Coaker recorded in his log that the *Adventure* was not conforming to the new standards. That vessel was commanded by Jacob Kean (Abram's nephew) and supplied by the merchant firm A.J. Harvey and Company.

Hard bread: a staple food for sealers.

Sealers from the *Nascopie* pull aboard a load of ice for cooking and drinking, ca. 1930.
MHA, PF-118.007

Harvey's also owned the *Newfoundland*, and it was failing to provide that crew with adequate food as well. Breakfast and most dinners aboard that vessel consisted of hard bread and tea. On Tuesdays, Thursdays, and Sundays, the men ate a warm dinner of salt pork and boiled duff. Fresh meat, pea soup, and soft bread were served only a few times.

Religion at the Floes

The shipboard service that Coaker recorded in his log on March 29 was not unusual. Religion played a large role in the sealers' lives, and similar scenes would have unfolded on all the other steamers in the fleet that day. Sunday meant that work stopped and worship began—no matter how many seals were on the ice.

The Newfoundland House of Assembly made Sunday sealing illegal in 1893. Any captain who broke that law would face a stiff fine or time in jail. Captain Arthur Jackman of the *Eagle* had to pay $2,000 in 1906 for making his men work on Sundays. But many sealers and some captains had been refusing to work on Sundays long before the legislation was passed—and they lost out in pelts and cash in the process. The issue finally erupted in public debate in April 1892, after 35 sealers aboard the steamer *Nimrod* were docked one-quarter of their pay for sitting out two Sundays that spring. Within days of the newspaper reports, MHA Henry Woods introduced an act to ban Sunday hunting in the House of Assembly. It was passed the following year.

$2,000 or Three Months

THE Sunday sealing case of John LeMessurier vs. Capt. Jackman, of the S.S. Eagle, for killing seals on Sunday was concluded to-day. Mr Furlong, K.C., moved that the case be dismissed on the grounds that there was no evidence against Capt. Jackman. The Judge did not agree with this, and sentenced the captain to pay the full penalty of $2,000, or in default, go to prison for three months. Mr. Furlong asked His Honor to state a case for the Supreme Court, to which the Judge agreed. Mr. John McCarthy for plaintiff.

Evening Telegram, April 30, 1906

The 1914 sealing legislation imposed fines of between $25 and $500 per offence, but this was poorly enforced. Despite Coaker's efforts and the occasional angry letter to the editor of the *Daily Mail* and other local newspapers, merchant firms did little to improve the sealers' diets, which did not change until well after the First World War.

To supplement the food that the merchant firms provided, almost every sealer brought his own stash of rolled oats and raisins to the floes. They mixed it with melted snow or the water that collected in depressions in the ice and sweetened it with molasses. Before too long, the men thought of little else but reaching the herds and enjoying some fresh meat: flippers, hearts, livers, blood—anything that could enhance their monotonous meals and provide much-needed protein and other nutrients.

On the Eve of Disaster

MR. COAKER'S LOG

March 30th —Took about 200 seals. In company with *Beothic*, *Eagle*, *Sagona* and *Fogota*. Fine day, but seals very scarce. Ice tight with a considerable swell. Court held on board at 8 p.m., Mosie Waterman being the first to answer to a charge. He was ably defended by Dr. Bunting. The sentence of the court being that the left side of his moustache should be shaved by Constables Lidstone and Norris. His counsel pleaded for suspended sentence, which was granted.

The next case being against N. Green. The charge was not proven but a minor offence being sustained, the sentence of the court was that he had to be taken to his bunk, his left boot and sock removed, his toes painted with molasses, and the sock and boot replaced, which sentence was carried out by Constables Lidstone and Norris.

PRISONER ACQUITTED

The third case being a charge against W. Humphries, for manslaughter, which was not proven. The complainant being charged by the court with false arrest was sentenced to have his left boot filled with water. The whole ship's company attended. Splendid order prevailed. Smoking was suspended and heads uncovered. N. Green and S. White were ably defended by G. Carter and Eli Mercer.

Another custom being sharing empty barrels, 100 applicants being made for one barrel. These barrels are filled with seal carcasses. The cook decided to dispose of the barrel today by ticket, and the ceremony of drawing was very interesting. Thirty-six was the successful number, which fell to the lot of A. Hapgood, of Port Blandford, who was immensely pleased with his good luck.

The *Newfoundland* picking up seal pelts in 1912. *The Rooms Provincial Archives Division, VA 164-28*

Westbury Kean

At 29, Westbury Kean was one of the youngest captains at the floes, but he was not inexperienced. He had been working at sea since he was 14 years old. He got his start at the Labrador fishery and eventually went on to skipper a vessel for his family's firm, A. Kean and Sons. Finally, in 1911, he became an ice captain. Westbury didn't have his master's certificate, but Harvey and Company gave him command of the *Newfoundland* anyway.

Being Abram Kean's son certainly helped him get that job, but Westbury would have to perform at the floes if he wanted to keep it—and especially if he wanted to command a steel ice-breaker. The first three springs went well. Westbury got along with the crew and brought home a respectable number of pelts despite the shortcomings of his old wooden-wall. But the 1914 disaster changed everything. He stayed away from the floes for years afterwards, skippering coastal steamers and vessels engaged in the fish trade. In 1918, he earned his master's certificate. Westbury returned to the seal hunt in 1921, when Bowring Brothers offered him command of the wooden-wall *Ranger*. He ended his sealing career in 1939 as captain of the *Imogene*, a powerful iron-clad. Westbury moved to the United States soon afterwards, and died at Merrick, New York, on January 20, 1974.

Two weeks into the hunt, the *Newfoundland* had little to show for it. Only about 400 ... the seals were nowhere in ...

... 1939.
... 58-10

... the *Stepha-* ... vessels were ... as no doubt ... formidable

... mained and ... rews would ... cided that if ... ed the next ... en to walk ... would not ... *ndland*, but ... ld let them ... ls.

Agreement entered into at St. John's Nfld., between Wesley Kean Master of the steamer Newfoundland, and the several persons whose names are signed hereto.

Witnesseth, that the several persons undersigned agreed to proceed on a sealing voyage in the said vessel and to serve in the several capacities set opposite their respective names. They shall come into service on the day of March, without further notice, or sooner if called upon, and proceed to sea whenever the master may deem fit. Each man shall assist in trimming coal and do any work in connection with the voyage required of him. Every man shall, in all respects, exert himself to the best of his ability for the good of the voyage, and be at all times obedient to the lawful commands of the master and officers; whether on board, at sea, on shore, or on the ice, in all respects, as if shipped on wages, and should any man neglect or be found incompetent for the proper performance of his duties in any respect (except by reason of sickness) he shall be entitled to only such share of seals as the master may allow him. Should any man be drunk or disorderly, or refuse to obey the lawful commands of the master or officer in charge before leaving port on the voyage he may be dismissed by the master, and shall not be entitled to any share of the seals taken on the voyage, or other compensation; nor shall any man be so entitled who shall absent himself after coming into service, at any time until the final termination of the voyage without leave of the master. Any man failing to proceed on the voyage after signing articles shall not be entitled to any share of the voyage. Any embezzlement or wilful or negligent loss or destruction of any part of the ship's cargo, stores or equipment shall be made good to the owners out of the earnings of the party so offending, or conniving at such offence, without prejudice to any other remedy which the owners may have for the same. In case of any gun or rifle being wilfully or carelessly lost or damaged during the voyage, the loss or damage shall be made good to the owners by deduction from the crew's share of seals. Engineers and Firemen shall not be required to go upon the ice, except by order of the master. In the event of the master named in this Agreement being prevented by sickness or other cause from proceeding upon or prosecuting the voyage, this Agreement shall be in all respects in force and binding as between the undersigned parties and the master who may be appointed in his stead.

In consideration of this Agreement being in all respects well and faithfully performed, the said crew are to receive as remuneration for their services at the final termination of the full voyage, (which it is declared, shall be when the seals are discharged and weighed off), every man an equal share or portion, according to the number of the crew, master, officers, engineers and firemen included, of one third of the value of the seals brought in and delivered from the vessel, being the catch of the said crew (after one full share of the net value of the cargo has been deducted for distribution amongst the officers as the captain may deem fit), (and one man's share for the firemen, to be equally divided between them in lieu of a man's share to captain), from which shall be deducted and retained the amount of account of each man, with the owners and supplying merchants. The supplying merchants do not bind themselves to give any outfit or crop to the crew, but in the event of such being issued, the prices charged shall be one-third over the retail cash prices of such articles issued, which one-third shall be deemed to be full compensation for the risk run, and any balance remaining unpaid by the said crew at the termination of the voyage shall be cancelled. It is agreed that the whole of the seals shall be landed immediately upon the arrival of vessel, and that the owners are to have the refusal of the crew's share of seals at the current price paid to crews of steamers.

If any man absents himself without the leave of the master or officer in charge whilst the seals are being landed, he shall incur a fine of two dollars per day for every day he is absent from or neglects such duty, the same shall be deducted from his share of the seals.

If any man shall sign a false name not his own and shall proceed in the said vessel personating or representing himself to be another, it shall be in the option of the master or suppliers to withhold from him any share of the

Ordered Overboard

A red sun crept over the icefields on the morning of Tuesday, March 31. George Tuff climbed high up the *Newfoundland*'s mast and into the barrel mounted near its top. He pointed his spyglass to the northwest and saw the *Stephano*, *Bonaventure*, and *Florizel* about 5 miles away. Their crews were already on the ice, fanning out in search of seals. The *Newfoundland* was firmly jammed. Tuff was frustrated, and so was Captain Westbury Kean.

Both men decided it was time to send the crew overboard. Tuff agreed to take the lead. As second hand, he was under no obligation to leave the vessel, but his 17 years of experience would come in handy on a long trek like this. Kean was relieved. He told Tuff to go to the *Stephano* and take orders from Abram Kean. He was certain his father would bring the *Newfoundland*'s men to the seals and then give them shelter for the night.

It would be a long hike over difficult ice, but at least the weather seemed fine—the breeze was soft and the ship's barometer signalled a fair day. Unfortunately, the *Newfoundland* did not have a thermometer on board or a wireless set for receiving weather reports. Some of the men decided to leave their heavy jackets behind, believing the extra bulk would only slow them down.

Starting at 7 a.m., 166 men scrambled over the *Newfoundland*'s sides and headed for the distant *Stephano*. It turned out to be a slog over some of the worst ice any of them had ever seen. Making matters worse, the *Stephano* was slowly steaming north, increasing the distance they had to walk. Tuff told them to mark a trail by blackening peaks of ice with the coal dust that clung to their mittens. He had been part

MR. COAKER'S LOG

SCATTERED SEALS

March 31st — East from Fogo about 30 miles early in the day. *Sagona*, *Eagle* and *Beothic* in company. Steaming through ice; a few scattered seals about. Ice poor for getting around on. Took a young hood seal alive on board. Have also two screachers alive on board. The hood seal is the most interesting of the three. The hood is about two days old. It has a beautiful skin. The hood seal sheds its white furry coat before pupping. A screacher is a harp seal whose mother perished after giving birth to the pup. It is consequently very small and devoid of fat matter. It is not killed by the sealers as it is valueless in their estimation. About ten in a thousand are screachers.

EAGERLY WANTED

Then there is the cat harp. This seal is eagerly sought by the sealer, as it is the seal that is dressed and known as the white coat. A cat white coat is so called because it was still-born. The fur of the still-born will not pull, i.e., the fur will remain in its natural state. A white coat born alive will shed its white coat.

The proportion of still-born harps (cats) would average about 10 in a thousand. Out of 18,000 young pelts on board there is about 50 cat skins, but all the cats were not brought on board, as in the morning men often pass by cats as it would be using up energy to carry a cat slung across the shoulders all day. The custom is to sling the cat across the shoulder and when once done it remains until the ship is reached. Consequently some men refuse to take a cat skin in the morning, unless they feel sure they will be picked by their ship within an hour or two, for a cat slung across a sealer's back interferes somewhat with the free movement of his arms in pelting seals.

VALUABLE PELTS

Each cat skin is worth at least one dollar, as there is a demand for them in a dressed form. The smaller the cat the more it is worth as a curiosity.

The early morning was clear at 10 a.m., indications of weather observable. At noon looked as if we would have snow storm, weather mild. At 1 p.m. snow thick, lost sight of men on ice near ship; snow cleared a little and all men taken on board. Captain kept men close to ship all morning. Snowing and blowing bitterly all evening.

At nightfall the wind was blowing a gale from the N. with snow. Real wintery night. Our men all on board at 4 p.m., when weather came on. Considerable swell all day. A stowaway on board ill with mumps and is confined to hospital.

A sealer for 17 years and a survivor of the 1898 *Greenland* disaster, George Tuff was 32 when he became the *Newfoundland*'s second hand in 1914. *ASCD, Coll.115 16.04.032*

In Their Own Words: Testimony from the Enquiry

George Tuff, Survivor

The Captain said, "George, ain't it hard to see that the men of these ships are in the seals and we can do nothing?" And I answered, "Do nothing, Captain? Heavens, we can walk there." The Captain said, "Will you go and lead the men, George?" I was glad to get the offer and said, "Yes, I will."

of the *Greenland*'s crew that had become stranded in 1898 and he had no desire to get lost again.

As the morning wore on, some of the sealers chatted uneasily about the weather. Dark clouds were gathering and sun hounds hung in the sky—small yellow discs that appear on either side of the sun and signal an approaching storm. At about 10 a.m., 34 men turned back for the *Newfoundland*. They knew the other sealers would call them cowards and that Westbury Kean would give them an earful, but something about the sky didn't seem right.

The other 132 sealers pressed on, reaching the *Stephano* at 11:30. By then it was beginning to snow and everyone was tired and hungry. Abram Kean slowed his steamer to a crawl so the men could climb aboard. He offered them hard bread and tea, but little else. Wasting no time, Kean steamed close to a herd of seals that lay about 2 miles southwest and ordered the men overboard. Pan about 1,500 pelts, he told Tuff, and then head back to the *Newfoundland*. There would be no sleeping aboard the *Stephano* that night.

The *Stephano*. It took the *Newfoundland* sealers about five hours to walk from their vessel to the *Stephano*. *MHA, PF-008.100*

Shock rippled through some of the men, but no one dared question the legendary Abram Kean. Tuff suggested they might be in for bad weather, but the ice master disagreed. That wasn't the only mistake Kean made that day. At 9 a.m., the *Stephano*'s barrel man had sighted the *Newfoundland*'s men on the ice for the first time. Both he and Kean assumed that was when they had left their vessel and that the *Newfoundland* was only a two-hour walk away, instead of five.

When Kean ordered the men overboard at noon, snow was falling and the wind was picking up. Everyone's heart sank as the *Stephano* steamed off to pick up its own crew working about 6 miles to the north. Tuff led the men toward the seals, but the weather quickly deteriorated. By 12:45, a thick veil of blowing snow had erased the rest of the world. It was time to turn back.

Captain Abram Kean in 1912.
The Rooms Provincial Archives Division, VA 107-9.1

Thomas Ryan, Survivor
When the crew left the *Newfoundland* on Tuesday morning, they had their usual clothing on; all hands had their overalls and jumpers on. All hands as far as I know had provisions. I had about six cakes of biscuit.

Edmund Short, One of the 34 who turned back
I turned back because I thought it was going to be stormy and I did not see anything ahead of me but death.

Josiah Holloway, Survivor
Before we went down I saw Capt. A. Kean on the bridge. I heard him say, "Hurry up boys, come aboard and get a mug-up." I had hard bread and butter and cold tea. I did not have time to eat it when the order was given to turn out again.... I could not see our ship when we got on the ice. It was too thick.

Frederick Yetman, *Stephano*'s Barrel Man
Between eight and nine o'clock I saw the *Newfoundland* crew coming towards us. It appeared to me as if they were just leaving their ship. The Captain was then on the bridge, and I told him the *Newfoundland*'s crew was just leaving her. I afterwards heard that they had left her at 7 o'clock and being up high on the rough ice, it appeared to me that they were just leaving their ship.

Ship registry data and archival photographs helped model-ship maker John H. Andela reconstruct the SS *Newfoundland* in 2011. *Courtesy John H. Andela*

Back on the *Newfoundland*, Westbury Kean had spent most of the morning in the barrel, keeping an eye on his men as they walked across the ice. At 10 a.m., he watched with irritation as 34 sealers turned back, and at 11:30 he was relieved to see the other 132 board the *Stephano*. Thick snow made it impossible to see much more after that, but he could finally relax, knowing that his father would take care of his men. At noon, he ordered the *Newfoundland*'s whistle blown to guide his 34 men home. It sounded until 1:30, when the last man scrambled on board.

Miles away from any vessel, 132 sealers were struggling through a worsening storm. Wind and snow bit at their faces and stung their eyes. They trudged through deepening snowdrifts and tried to keep balance on unsteady ice pans that dipped and rolled over stormy seas. Ice water penetrated their boots. Worse was the occasional slip that sent a man waist-deep into freezing seas before his companions pulled him to safety. They had to keep moving.

Finally, at about 2 p.m., the men spotted a black smear of coal on a peak of ice—it was their morning trail. For a hope-filled hour or two they tried desperately to retrace their steps to the *Newfoundland*, but it was futile. Blowing snow soon erased their markings and strong waves moved the pans in every direction, rearranging the floes beneath their feet. Disoriented and blinded by a curtain of snow, they were hopelessly lost.

As darkness inked the sky, Tuff ordered the men to stop and build shelters. It was just after 5 p.m. and the blizzard was in full force, with no signs of weakening. No single ice pan was large enough to accommodate all of the men, so they had to split into smaller groups. Tuff took charge of one and master watches Arthur Mouland and Thomas Dawson the others.

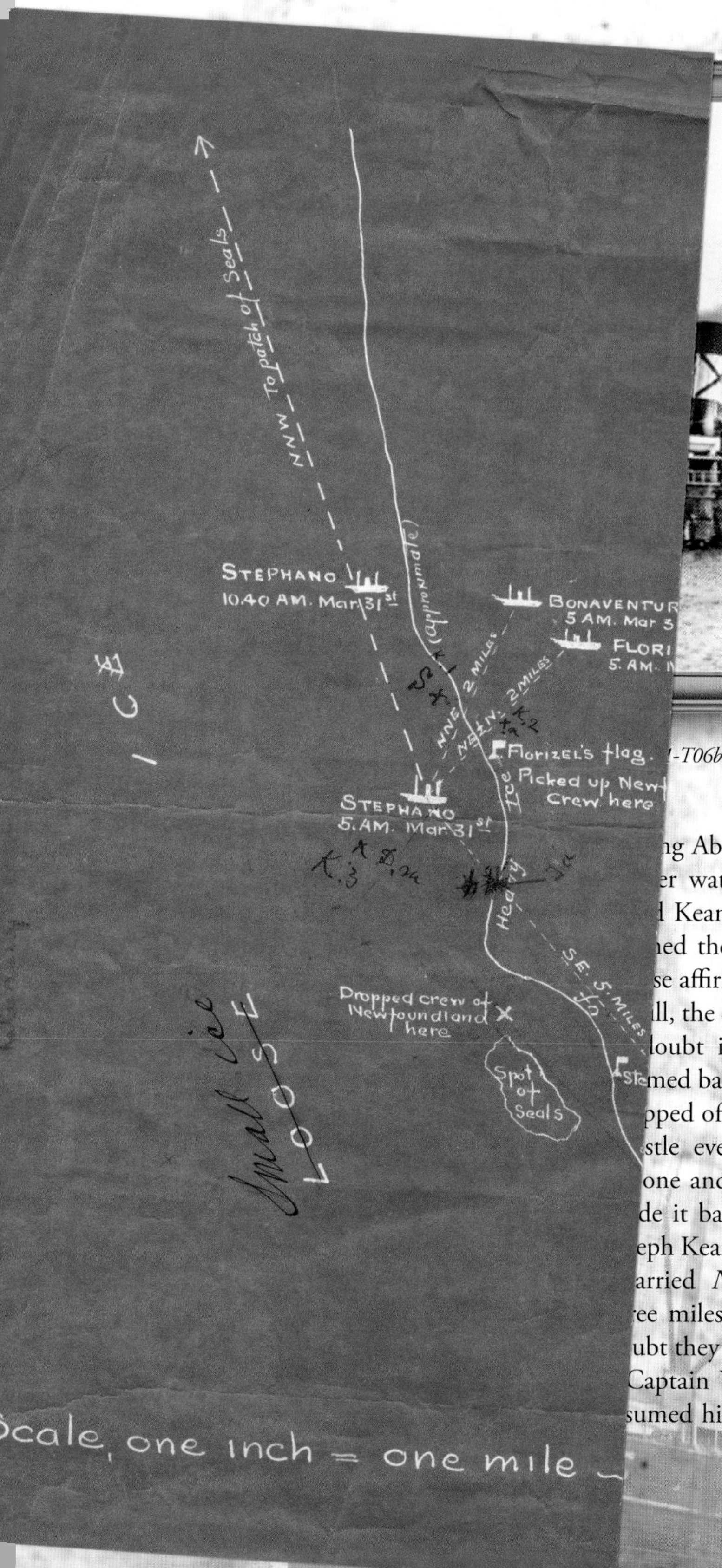

-T06b

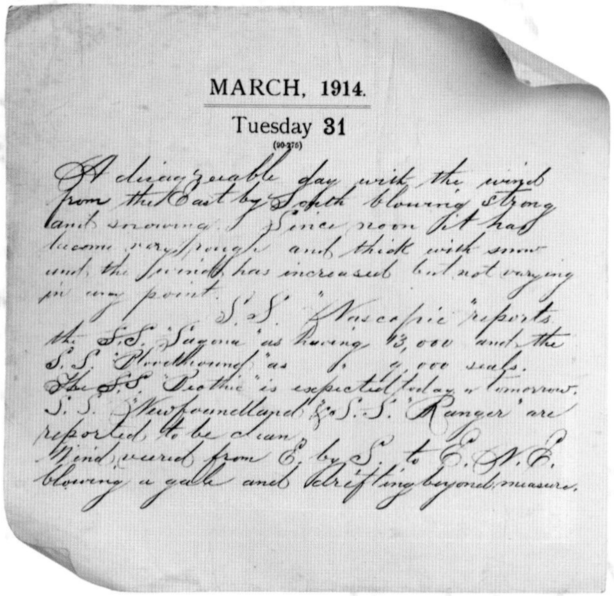
MARCH, 1914.

Tuesday 31

A disagreeable day with the wind from the East by South blowing strong and snowing. Since noon it has become very rough and thick with snow and the wind has increased but not varying in any point.

S.S. "Nascopie" reports the S.S. "Sagona" as having 3,000 and the S.S. "Bloodhound" as 4,000 seals. The S.S. "Beothic" is expected today or tomorrow. S.S. "Newfoundland" & S.S. "Ranger" are reported to be clean.

Wind veered from E. by S. to E.N.E. blowing a gale and drifting beyond measure.

A weather report and sealing update for March 31, 1914, as reported in a business diary belonging to the Bonavista merchant firm of James Ryan Ltd. *MHA, James Ryan Limited (Bonavista) fonds*

ng Abram Kean's judgment. When er watch Garland Gaulton finally l Kean if he thought the men had hed the *Newfoundland*, he received se affirmative reply.

ll, the question likely planted a seed loubt in Kean's mind, because he med back to where the *Stephano* had pped off the men, blowing the ship's stle every five minutes. Kean saw one and assumed that the men had de it back safely. He wired Captain eph Kean of the *Florizel* at 8:19 p.m.: arried *Newfoundland*'s crew within ee miles ship before noon, have no ubt they are aboard their own ship."

Captain Westbury Kean, meanwhile, sumed his men were safely aboard either the *Stephano* or the *Florizel*, but he had no way of contacting his father and brother to find out if that was true. The old wooden-wall was still firmly jammed in the floes and miles of impenetrable pack ice separated it from the iron-clads working to the north. He went to bed cheered by the thought that his men had panned a substantial number of pelts that he could take back to St. John's.

Captain Joseph Kean. On the night of March 31, 1914, Joseph Kean received word from his father, Captain Abram Kean of the *Stephano*, that the *Newfoundland*'s men had returned to their vessel. *ASCD, Coll. 203 5.55.001*

Second Day on the Ice

MR. COAKER'S LOG

BLOWING GALE

April 1st — Blowing a gale from the North during early part of the day veering to N.W. in the evening, with very little abatement in the wind. Ice very tight. Ship made but little progress. Freezing hard. A real February Day. Took two or three hood seals. *Eagle* and *Adventure* sighted about 4 p.m. about five miles off.

Held a gramophone concert in the officers' quarters after tea. Uncle Darius Hall sang a song entitled "The Bold Hero." Levi Green sang "Come all ye jolly ice hunters," and David Rodgers sang "On the Banks of the Clyde." Each song was well received. That sung by Levi Green was composed by a sealer on board the *Leopard* the spring Captain Bob Fowlow secured so many white coats. Mosie Waterman told one of his remarkable "big fib" stories. The concert ended at 10 p.m.

In the fore hold "Greenspond" held a ball and danced to the music of an accordion, loaned by a fireman, until it was time to turn in. Ship supposed to be about 40 miles South East of the Funks. The ice must have drifted two miles an hour. The Marconi reports the *Stephano* about 20 miles distant.

STORMY WINTRY DAY

This is a stormy wintry day, but the boys of the *Nascopie* only knew of the storm when appearing on deck. All was contentment and enjoyment under decks. Such is life on a steel ice hunter on a wintry day, blowing a hurricane, on the bosom of the mighty angry Atlantic.

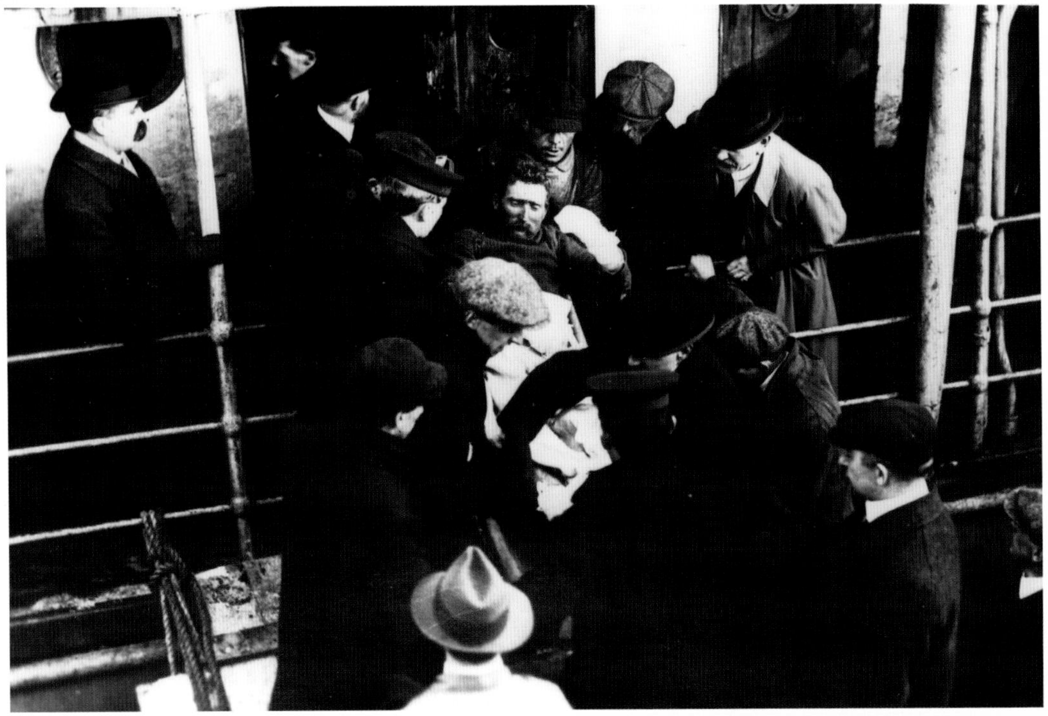

Thomas Dawson of Bay Roberts arrives at St. John's on April 4, 1914. He was a master watch on the *Newfoundland* and in charge of about 50 or 60 sealers, including one of the first fatalities: Thomas Jordan of Pouch Cove. Dawson lost both of his feet to frostbite. *ASCD, Coll. 115 16.04.048*

The cozy scene that Coaker described aboard the *Nascopie* could not have been more different from that which the *Newfoundland*'s men were experiencing out on the floes. The storm that began on Tuesday afternoon raged all night and well into the next day. It assaulted the men with fierce winds, ice pellets, and sub-zero temperatures. Their makeshift shelters were of little use.

They jumped and stomped, huddled close, and took turns acting as windbreaks for the others. It was a losing battle. Numbness crept over their bodies and ice encased their clothes. One of the men, Jesse Collins, lost all feeling in his lips after biting away the ice that sealed his friends' eyelids shut; their frozen fingers were useless to wipe it away. Some men sang songs to keep their spirits up, others prayed, and a few grew still.

"About 10 o'clock that night the first man died, Thomas Jordan of Pouch Cove," Richard McCarthy later testified at the enquiry into the disaster. McCarthy was on a pan with about 50 or 60 men under master watch Thomas Dawson. Jordan slipped into the ocean. Two other sealers pulled him out, but the shock and cold killed him soon afterwards. By daylight, 14 or 15 men in McCarthy's group were dead. It was a similar story on the other pans.

LOG BOOK

OF THE

S/S. "Stephano"

~~From the Port of~~ New York

~~To~~ Halifax N.S. and St Johns N.F.

Commencing

Ending

LOG of the S/S "Stephano"

From St John's N.F. **Towards** Icefields

CHIEF OFFICER'S LOG

Hr	Knots	Fathoms	Direction	Force	Sail Set	Lee Way	Barometer	Temperature Air	Temperature Water	Deviation

REMARKS, &c. Tuasday 31st day of March 1914

1
2 Light Southerly breeze and veering
3 easterly fine clear weather
4 5.10 A.M Ship underway ice slack making
5 good progress Barometer 29/75
6 6. A.M all men on ice panning seals
7 Ship picking up pans
8 "Florizel" and "Bon" in companey Bell and
9 "N.F.L.D" in sight
10 11.20 A.M "N.F.L.D" crew walked on board had
11 mugup and went on ice again about 11.50 am
12

1 Noon wind increasing from S.E with light
2 snow Barometer 29/50 and falling
3
4 3.30 P.M wind increasing to storm with
5 blinding snow Ships horn kept going
6 "Florizel" picked up Maney of our crew came
7 alongside about 4.30 and put them on Board
8 Ship continues picking up pans
9 4. P.M wind E.S.E with heavy snow blizzard and
10 turning very coald
11 6. P.M wind increasing and veering to N.N.E
12 Ship stopped and burnt down ice very tight

BEARING & DISTANCE AT NOON. Barometer 29/40 Thermometer 16 above zero

COURSE	DISTANCE	Difference Latitude	Departure	Latitude by Account	Latitude Observed	Difference of Longitude	Longitude by Account	Longitude by Chronometer	Longitude Observed	Variation	Distance per Patent

ON THE LOOK-OUT From	To	NAME	LANTERNS HUNG OUT From	To

Mate. A. Kean Master

Most of the sealers stayed put on

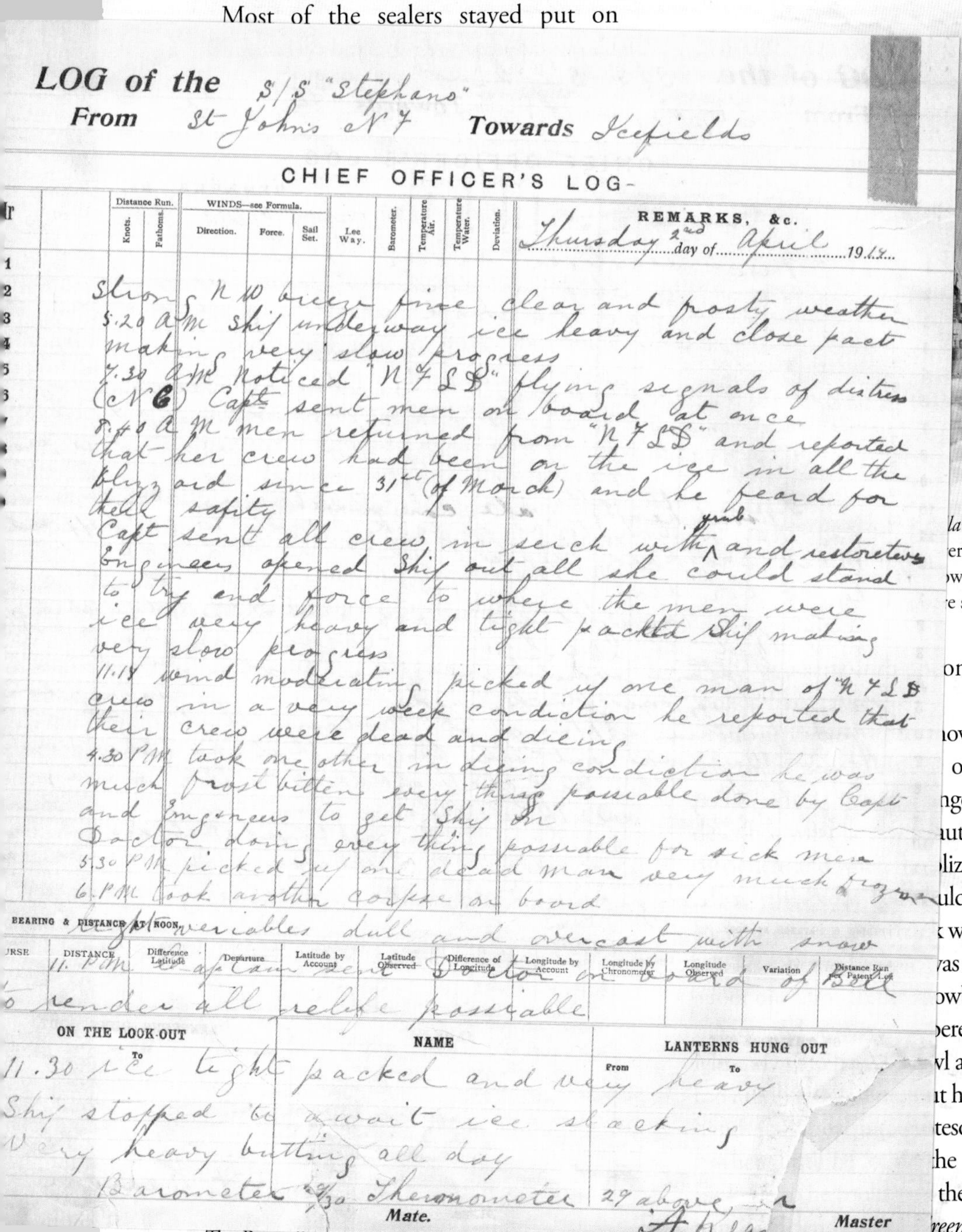
LOG of the S/S "Stephano"
From St John's N F **Towards** Icefields

CHIEF OFFICER'S LOG-

REMARKS, &c. Thursday 2nd day of April 1914

Strong N W breeze fine clear and frosty weather
5.20 AM Ship underway ice heavy and close pact
making very slow progress
7.30 AM Noticed "N F L D" flying signals of distress
(N 6) Capt sent men on board at once
8.40 AM men returned from "N F L D" and reported
that her crew had been on the ice in all the
blizzard since 31st (of March) and he feard for
their safety
Capt sent all crew in serch with food and restoretives
Engineers opened Ship out all she could stand
to try and force to where the men were
ice very heavy and tight packed Ship making
very slow progress
11.15 wind moderating picked up one man of "N F L D"
crew in a very week condiction he reported that
their crew were dead and dieing
4.30 PM took one other in dieing condiction he was
much frost bitten every thing possable done by Capt
and Engineers to get Ship in
Doctor doing every thing possable for sick men
5.30 PM picked up one dead man very much frozen
6 PM took another corpse on board

BEARING & DISTANCE AT NOON

Night veriables dull and overcast with snow
11 PM Captain sent Doctor on board of Bell
to render all relefe possable

ON THE LOOK-OUT / NAME / LANTERNS HUNG OUT

11.30 ice tight packed and very heavy
Ship stopped to await ice slacking
Very heavy butting all day
Barometer 29/30 Thermometer 29 above

Mate. A. Kean Master

The Ryan diary reported exceptionally bad weather on April 1, 1914: "With last night's E.N.E. blizzard and today's hurricane from the North we have upon us the worst coarsest day for the Winter." *MHA, James Ryan Limited (Bonavista) fonds*

...laventure, jammed in ice off Fogo, 1914.
...ere worried that the *Newfoundland*'s men
...wn vessel, but Captain Abram Kean was
...e safe. *MHA, PF-320.001*

...onsciousness. Their frozen bodies

...nove to stay warm, but everywhere
... over corpses. Sometimes it was a
...nger. Survivor Cecil Mouland later
...author Cassie Brown: "A lot of them
...blizzard got really bad, they got drift-
...uld look over there and see a hand
...with the mitt on, or the fellow who
...was blowing around in the snow and
...owbank."

...ered an elderly sealer named Ezra
...wl across the ice because his legs were
...t he had lost his mittens and his bare
...tesque claws. Mouland searched eve-
...he mitts. He sliced them open with
... them over the old sealer's misshapen
...*reenland* survivor, but he died on the
ice that spring. His body was never found.

The survivors clung to the hope that rescuers were scouring the icefields for them. Surely a ship's whistle would soon penetrate the wind and guide them to safety. But there was no search party. Abram Kean was certain that the men had made it back to the *Newfoundland* and Westbury Kean was certain they were aboard the *Stephano* or *Florizel*. Westbury's only concerns were his jammed vessel and the loss of yet another workday, this time to the storm.

Cecil Mouland (pictured right, with an unidentified man) and his ticket to board the *Newfoundland*. Mouland was a teenager when he went to the ice floes for the first time in 1914. He said that thinking of his fiancée, Jessie Collins, helped him survive the disaster. The two were later married. *ASCD, Coll. 115 16.04.098; MHA, MF-0139*

Every passing minute placed the men in greater danger. They were freezing and they were dying. The storm had created giant snowdrifts in some places and exposed large patches of slippery ice in others. It was hard to judge which was solid ice and which was slush. Many men fell into the water. Some were pulled back by their companions, only to die a few moments later.

Everyone was weak and exhausted. Their legs were numb and wobbly, their minds unfocused. Even George Tuff began to crack under the pressure. He openly criticized Abram Kean for putting them on the ice in an approaching storm. "All of us will be lost," he cried out at one point.

But there was a surge of hope around 3:30 that afternoon when some of the sealers spotted the *Bellaventure* about 2 miles away. The storm was finally weakening and they had a clearer view of the icefields. Tuff, master watch Arthur Mouland, and a small group of other men headed for the steamer as fast as they could.

"I went off towards her, and in doing so I had to pass through all the rest of the gang," Tuff testified at the enquiry. "The first pan I met was all dead men. I did not notice the number particularly but there might have been a dozen or more there. I then reached the pan with the live men on it. I told them to cheer up, that the steamer would be here in a half hour's time."

Sealers from the various vessels bring the frozen dead to the *Bellaventure* on April 2 or 3, 1914. *ASCD, Coll. 115 16.04.038*

Mouland came close enough to the *Bellaventure* to see a man on its bulkhead. Full of hope, he scrambled up a high ridge of ice and waved furiously. No one saw him. He stared, devastated, as the *Bellaventure* turned and steamed in the opposite direction. Perhaps no one was looking for them after all. His suspicion was

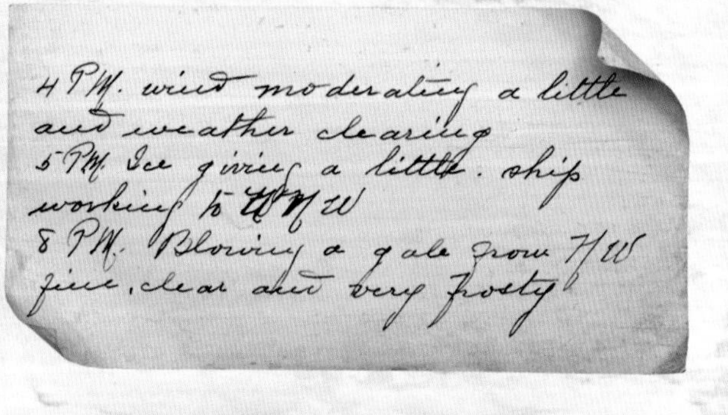

4 PM. wind moderating a little
and weather clearing
5 PM. Ice giving a little. ship
working to WNW
8 PM. Blowing a gale from NW
fine, clear and very frosty

An excerpt from the *Newfoundland*'s logbook on April 1, 1914, reports that the vessel broke free from the pack ice at about 5 p.m. and started steaming north-northwest. No one on board knew that a group of survivors was only an hour's walk away. *The Rooms Provincial Archives Division, GN 121-51*

In Their Own Words: Testimony from the Enquiry

George F. Shecklen, *Stephano*

On Wednesday morning I remember asking Captain Kean what he thought of the *Newfoundland*'s men, and he said, "Oh, undoubtedly they are back on their own ship."

Richard McCarthy, Survivor

Shortly after I got on the pan my bunk mate died, Albert Kelloway. We then left and went over to another pan where there was about 20 or 30 men. Tuff and Jones were there. I heard Tuff saying, smacking his hands, "'Tis old Kean's fault, 'tis old Kean's fault."

Thomas Mouland, Survivor

The weather had continued stormy up to 3 or 4 o'clock on Wednesday evening. The wind changed during Tuesday night and it got cold, and continued getting colder.

A 1914 collage of the sealing vessels *Bellaventure*, under Captain Randell, and *Newfoundland*, under Captain Westbury Kean. The stranded sealers sighted both vessels during their second day on the ice but could not attract the attention of anyone on board. *MHA, PF-055.2-F50*

George Tuff, Survivor

I got upon a pinnacle and looked to windward and I saw the *Bellaventure*; I allowed her to be two miles away. I said, "Boys, cheer up, we are all right." I said, "We'll be aboard a steamer in less than any time, that man will see us and he will come to us." … All at once she slewed around and went away from us, and it was pretty hard for me to tell the men that she was not coming.

Sydney Jones, Survivor

One of the men who was with me, Henry Dowden, died about five minutes after the *Bellaventure* turned her stern on us. I was holding him up and when he died I laid him down. I only saw four men dying on the ice.

George Tuff, Survivor

Now it was after sunset. I allowed I was two miles from the *Newfoundland* and she was after getting loose, and steaming in the direction nearly away from us. I then said it remains for us to fix away a place for us to die, I suppose. Everyone as far as I could learn was waiting their end.

shared by the other sealers, who also watched the receding steamer from their ice pans more than a mile away. There was no way they could cross that that distance with nightfall only about an hour away.

Mouland's heart soon leaped for a second time when he spotted a column of black smoke rising about 4 miles to the south. It had to be the *Newfoundland*, still jammed where they had left it yesterday morning. Mouland and a small group of men struck out for the steamer. Darkness had fallen by the time they were close enough for the barrel man to see them, but that was of little concern—the *Newfoundland* was easy enough to see with all of its lights on. All they had to do was keep on walking.

Hope strengthened their bodies and sharpened their minds. It allowed them to push through snowdrifts and cross broken ice. Then the impossible happened. With only an hour's walk to go, the *Newfoundland* somehow broke free of the pack ice that had trapped it for days. No one could believe their eyes: not only was the vessel moving, it was steaming away from them. There was no chance of catching it. The *Newfoundland* was moving too fast and forever increasing the distance they would have to travel.

Could anyone survive a second night on the floes?

RESCUE

MR. COAKER'S LOG

April 2nd — Fine day; wind West. Met the *Diana* at 9 a.m. Several of *Diana's* men on board. Reports very bad cooking on board whole spring, and quite a lot of dissatisfaction. No brewse, no fresh beef and no canned beef. Bread only twice each week, and uneatable, being sour. Flour very bad, can't make good bread from it. No duff on April 1, being duff day. The chief cook is named Hr. Abbott. He should never be allowed to sail in a sealing steamer as cook. More care must be exercised in selecting the chief cooks for the crews. Captains will have to be hailed before the courts if they do not see that the cooks supply food as provided by law. The regulations can be carried out easily, as proved on board the *Nascopie*, where the food supplied exceeded what is provided by the new law.

EASY TO COOK

One of the easiest meals to cook is the brewse. It takes three quarters of a bag of bread on board of the *Nascopie* for a meal of brewse. Our cook has a boiler with a double bottom and brewse is cooked as easily as a woman cooks it at home.

The men on board the *Diana* are furious over the treatment accorded them, and judging by the statements made to me, Capt. Barbour will have to answer before the courts for breaches of the sealing law in reference to the supply of food.

At 10 a.m. our operator picked up a message from *Florizel* en route to St. John's, reporting *Newfoundland* disaster, which was followed by other reports confirming the same. The news caused tremendous excitement and sympathy on board.

The ship was headed at full pressure for the area where our captain supposed *Newfoundland* to be. The *Adventure* reported to us, intimating that they could see *Newfoundland* with flag half-mast. The ice was as tight as it could be forced together and of a very heavy nature, being chiefly Arctic ice. The ship kept butting continuously. At 4 p.m. the *Adventure* was four miles distant from us, the *Beothic* about six, the *Florizel* about eight, and the *Stephano* and *Newfoundland* about seven. The *Bellaventure* about six. The *Stephano* was nearest to the *Newfoundland*.

If 1,000 men were on the ice dying we could offer no aid. The mighty powers of Nature had brought about conditions that the most powerful ship could not force.

All day our crew waited silently for news by the wireless. Men huddled together and talked in whispers about the awful calamity that had overtaken the poor chaps belonging to the *Newfoundland*. Some of our crew were fathers, with sons amongst the number sailing in the *Newfoundland*. Some had brothers on board.

The second night on the ice was one long unbroken nightmare. Hope of rescue that had sustained the men was gone now. All that remained was a frozen expanse that swallowed men whole. The storm was over, but the wind was strong and cold. Death came quickly. Some men died praying, others died standing. It could even happen mid-step—one second someone was walking and talking, the next he fell down, a frozen corpse. Everyone who lived had to watch someone die.

"It was really a tragedy to see those strapping men topple over just like a log," Cecil Mouland later recalled. "They'd freeze and topple over. And some fellows that didn't want to die, you know, they really died hard. Some fellows that had family at home and they fought until the very last minute to live because of their loved ones at home. I think when they died, they really died hard. I saw them struggling until the last minute, you know, trying to keep alive. They did everything to keep alive, but had to give up."

Worn out, afraid, and freezing, the survivors' minds began to break under the strain. Hallucination mixed with reality. Some men saw rescuers coming toward them with kettles of tea, others saw a steamer breaking through the ice. A few even saw their own homes in the icefields. They'd run to the door and knock madly, only to discover that they were pounding their fists on a peak of ice. Some men chased

Awful Disaster On the Icefields

Fifty Men Dead and Dying of the S. S. Newfoundland found by s. s. Bellaventure---One-third of Crew from Saint John's East---Extent of Disaster not Known---Ships Hurrying to Assistance ---Harvey's Wire for Particulars.

Evening Telegram, April 2, 1914

HARD WORK FOR THE TWO SURGEONS

Were Veritable Angels of Mercy to the Suffering on the Bellaventure.

WORKED FOR HOURS WITHOUT REFRESHMENT

One Collapsed From Nervous Strain When the Relief Ship Reached Port.

Evening Herald, April 2, 1914

Rescuers help an unidentified *Newfoundland* survivor board the *Bellaventure* on the morning of April 2, 1914. According to the photo's caption, he "died on deck of exhaustion." *ASCD, Coll. 115 16.04.040*

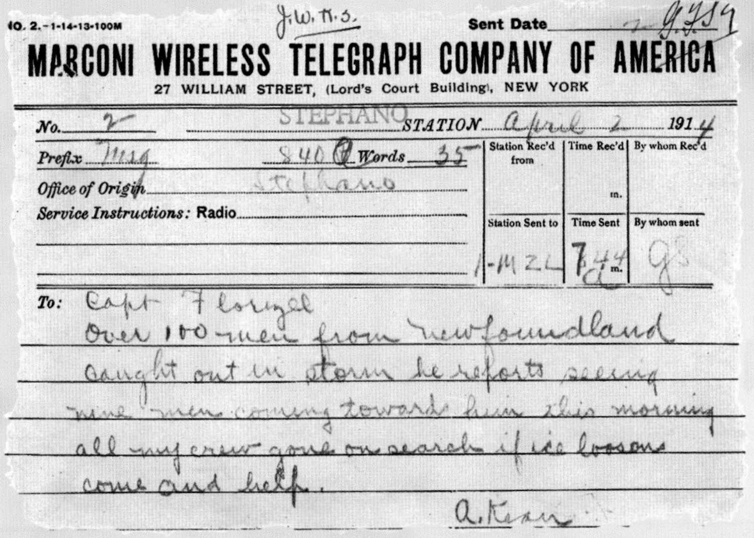

NO. 2.-1-14-13-100M J.W.H.S. Sent Date ... 9759

MARCONI WIRELESS TELEGRAPH COMPANY OF AMERICA

27 WILLIAM STREET, (Lord's Court Building), NEW YORK

No. 2 STEPHANO STATION April 2 1914

Prefix Msg 840 Words 35

Office of Origin Stephano

Service Instructions: Radio

Station Rec'd from	Time Rec'd	By whom Rec'd
	m.	
Station Sent to	**Time Sent**	**By whom sent**
1-MZL	7.44	G.S.

To: Capt Florizel
Over 100 men from Newfoundland
caught out in storm he reports seeing
nine men coming towards him this morning
all my crew gone on search if ice loosens
come and help.

A. Kean

Captain Abram Kean sent this telegram to his son Captain Joseph Kean of the *Florizel* on the morning of April 2, 1914. The captains of the *Stephano, Florizel,* and *Bellaventure* kept in close wireless contact all day to update one another of rescue efforts. *The Rooms Provincial Archives Division, GN 121-49, Despatch #2*

their hallucinations right off the edge and into the water.

Several miles to the north, the survivors saw something that wasn't a hallucination—the twinkling lights of the *Stephano*, *Newfoundland*, and a few other vessels burning down for the night. But the men could just as easily reach the stars in the sky as they could the steamers on the horizon. Seeing the lights only added to the torture, a horrible reminder that rescue was just out of grasp.

The *Newfoundland* had ground its way to within 2 miles of the *Stephano* before getting jammed in the ice again. Westbury Kean was anxious to reach his father's steamer and find out how many seals his men had panned, but it was too late to send anyone over by foot. He would just have to wait until morning. The other captains also looked forward to the sunrise, when their crews could return to the hunt after losing a full day to the storm.

MR. COAKER'S LOG

ANXIOUS TIME

I passed the morning in the top cabin anxious to hear the latest news by wireless. In the evening I spent most of the time with the men. The one prominent feature that I noted was the universal cry of captain, officers and men to do away with panning seals, as that system is responsible for most of the risks to life now experienced.

Captain Barbour told me that there would not have been a *Greenland* disaster had there been no practice of panning seals. The practice must be annihilated. I had a minor experience of this the other evening. I with about 60 men spent an anxious hour or two owing to our ship having gone out of sight to pick up pans [of seal pelts] and men, with thick weather soon after set in, but fortunately for us it was a mist instead of snow. The incident brought home to me the amount of risk to life incurred by the present methods of sealing.

WAITING PARTICULARS

We must await full particulars 'ere we decide who or what is responsible for this last and greatest disaster known in the history of the seal fishery.

Our ship kept butting without ceasing. The captain spent the whole day and night on the bridge, but alas poor progress was made. Our doctor was especially anxious to reach the *Bellaventure* as he may be of some use in alleviating the sufferings of those who had been rescued.

The ship steamed all night; ice conditions remaining unchanged. Progress about two miles during the night. Continually butting at highest pressure.

The first rays of sunlight revealed a heart-wrenching scene. The living crawled and staggered across the ice, some of them delirious, some still lucid. Many of the survivors were badly frostbitten. A few, including George Tuff, were ice-blind and could barely see. Perhaps it was just as well, because all around them lay bodies. The dead now outnumbered the living and their numbers were growing.

A few miles to the north lay the *Newfoundland*, *Stephano*, *Florizel*, and *Bellaventure*. Tuff, Arthur Mouland, and a group of men decided to walk toward the *Newfoundland*. It was farther away than the other vessels, but it was also the slowest and they worried that the fleet would steam away again. Another small group headed for the closer *Bellaventure*. Most of the other men stayed put. A few wandered off, hallucinating.

At 6 a.m., Westbury Kean was in the *Newfoundland's* barrel, his spyglass glued on the *Stephano* to the north. Where were his men? They should be on the ice by now. He turned to survey the icefields. When he pointed his spyglass to the southwest, he saw a small group of men, about 2 miles away, reeling and stumbling toward the *Newfoundland*. The horrible truth became immediately clear. His men had spent two nights and days on the ice in some of the worst weather he had ever experienced at the ice floes. How many were still alive?

Kean flew down the mast. Desperate to help, but lacking any flares or wireless equipment, he raised the only distress signal he could—a blue and white flag with a black basket underneath. Hopefully the other vessels would soon see it and send over men to investigate. The *Newfoundland's* crew scrambled overboard to help the approaching survivors.

The *Stephano* was the first to spot the distress signal. Two of its men hurried across the ice and their arrival confirmed what Westbury Kean had already assumed: the *Newfoundland's* men were not on board the *Stephano* and no one had seen them since noon on Tuesday. The *Stephano's* men rushed back to Abram Kean with news of the disaster. He ordered everyone overboard to search for survivors.

They took provisions—blankets, food, tea, rum, kindling, matches, anything that might help.

At around the same time, another group of *Newfoundland* survivors had finally made it to the *Bellaventure*. Captain Robert Randell was shocked by their news. At least 50 men were dead, they told him, and dozens more were still out there on the ice, waiting for rescue. His crew immediately joined the other search parties. The three iron-clads in the area—the

Rescuers return to the *Bellaventure* with dead and injured sealers.
MHA, PF-345.011

In Their Own Words: Testimony from the Enquiry

Westbury Kean, Master of the *Newfoundland*

I suddenly caught sight of nine men walking towards the *Newfoundland* and it occurred to me right then what had happened—that the men had got adrift and nobody knew what had happened or that they were out.

Arthur Abbott, Survivor

... at daylight on Thursday the men who were alive started to go towards her [the *Bellaventure*]. There were 25 dead men on our pan at this time, I think. I could not see very well as I was blind. I did not go towards her as I was blind, and I remained on the pan 'til I was picked up.

Westbury Kean, Master of the *Newfoundland*

We took the survivors which had reached our ship below, stripped them, put on warm clothing, gave them stimulants, and did everything that suggested itself to us. All these men lived.

LOG of the S. S. Newfoundland

From Wesleyville Towards Sealfishery

PATT. No. 8

CHIEF OFFICER'S LOG.

HOURS.	DISTANCE RUN. Knots.	Fathoms.	WINDS—See Formula. Direction.	Force.	Sail Set.	Lee Way.	Barometer.	Temperature Air.	Temperature Water.	Deviation.	REMARKS, &c.

Thursday April 2nd 1914

Begins with fine weather and fresh breeze

4 A.M. began steaming towards S/S Stephano to recover part of crew which were believed to be on board her. 6 A.M. some men were seen on the Ice walking towards us. and assistance was sent out to them 8 A.M. Second H and Tuff and some others were taken on board and reported that they with the remainder of crew left the Stephano on Tuesday afternoon to pan seals. Thick weather and a gale of wind prevented them from getting on board ships. all the men returned are frostbitten and reports many frozen to death.

Distress signals were hoisted and S/S Stephano and Bellaventure began seaching the Ice for men.

Bellaventure reported having picked up sixty of our crew at noon and Stephano one. Ice close and heavy. ships not making any headway.

8 P.M. light breeze from S.E. clear weather and overcast sky

BEARING AND DISTANCE AT NOON

COURSE.	DISTANCE.	Difference Latitude.	Departure.	Latitude by Account.	Latitude Observed.	Difference of Longitude.	Longitude by Account.	Longitude by Chronometer.	Longitude Observed.	Variation.	Distance Run per Patent Log.
					N 48.32			W 52.17			

ON THE LOOK OUT. NAME. LANTERNS HUNG OUT.

FROM	TO	NAME	FROM	TO
" Carefully attended to			" Sunset	" Sunrise
"	"		"	"
"	"		"	"
"	"		"	"
"	"		"	"
"	"		"	"

Master.

Mate.

LOG of the *S. S. Newfoundland*

From *Icefields* Towards *St Johns* **PATT. No. 8**

CHIEF OFFICER'S LOG.

HOURS.		DISTANCE RUN. Knots.	Fathoms	WINDS—See Formula. Direction.	Force.	Sail Set.	Lee Way.	Barometer.	Temperature Air.	Temperature Water.	Deviation.	REMARKS, &c.
												Friday April 3rd 1914
1 A.M.												*Begins with dull sky and*
2												*thick weather*
3												
4				*N/E*	*4*							*4 A.M. Do Do*
5												
6												
7												
8				*N*	*4*			*29.20*				*8 A.M. weather clearing*
9												*9 .. S/S Stephano steamed*
10												*up alongside. having on*
11												*board two of our crew alive*
12								*29.45*				*and two dead. which were*
1 P.M.												*transferred to the S/S Bellaventure*
2												*which also steamed up near*
3	*WSW*											*us.*
4								*29.60*				*After calling the roll all sick*
5												*men on board were transferred*
6												*to the Bellaventure.*
7												*3 P.M. got underweigh*
8	*WSW*			*NW*	*5*			*29.70*				*4 P.M. spoke to S/S Florizel*
9												*mod breeze Northerly. dull sky and*
10												*spitting snow.*
11												*8 P.M. fresh breeze N.W. and dull sky*
12												*so ends the day*

BEARING AND DISTANCE AT NOON

COURSE.	DISTANCE.	Difference Latitude.	Departure.	Latitude by Account.	Latitude Observed.	Difference of Longitude.	Longitude by Account.	Longitude by Chronometer.	Longitude Observed.	Variation.	Distance Run per Patent Log.
				N 48=12			*W 52=20*				

ON THE LOOK OUT. FROM	TO	NAME.	LANTERNS HUNG OUT. FROM	TO
" *Carefully*	"	*attended to*	" *Sunset*	" *Sunrise*
"	"		"	"
"	"		"	"
"	"		"	"
"	"		"	"
"	"		"	"

_______________ Master. _______________ Mate.

Bellaventure, *Stephano*, and *Florizel*—stayed in close contact by wireless for the rest of the day.

Captain Joseph Kean of the *Florizel* sent word to St. John's: "Fear terrible disaster; *Newfoundland*'s crew caught out in last blizzard, *Stephano* and *Bellaventure* sending men searching. *Bellaventure* found 50 men dead and dying. Ice terribly tight, we are helpless to render any assistance as yet but will proceed to her assistance first opportunity ... Both Father and myself in terrible way. Wes, poor fellow, in awful state. This is where wireless would have saved catastrophe if on all ships."

Almost every vessel in the fleet that had a wireless now knew of the disaster. Like the *Nascopie*, many of the steamers carried friends and relatives of the *Newfoundland*'s men. They waited anxiously for news. All over the floes, steamers slowly pushed their way toward the disaster site. Most were too far away to be of any help and thick ice slowed their progress.

But the *Bellaventure* was at the heart of the tragedy. Powerful and maneuverable, the iron-clad prowled the icefields on its grim mission. "Our ship continued until about 3 p.m. picking up the bodies of the live men," Captain Randell later told the enquiry. "They were coming in twos and threes all this time with squads of our men helping them. At three o'clock there were 34 men on board. Several could not walk and were brought on stretchers. Most of them were in pretty bad condition. The second hand had directed our men to gather together the dead bodies and put them on pans so as we would have no bother in picking them. These I picked up between 3 and 4 p.m. until we had onboard 58 bodies."

By the time darkness fell, 55 survivors were on board either the *Bellaventure*, *Stephano*, *Florizel*, or *Newfoundland*. Most were on the *Bellaventure*, where druggist Harold Smith worked tirelessly to soothe the patients with what little supplies were on hand. Many of the men were in agony. Severe frostbite maimed their bodies and left their skin blistered and purple. There would certainly be amputations when they reached St. John's. Smith breathed a sigh of relief when the *Stephano* finally steamed close enough at about 10 p.m. that its doctor could join him.

By then, all of the survivors and most of the bodies were on board. It was time to burn down for the night. The captains of the three iron-clads agreed to converge on the *Newfoundland* at daybreak to count the living and the dead.

Richard McCarthy, Survivor

I went down in the cabin with John Hiscock. I heard Capt. Wes Kean say, "Is that you John Hiscock?" And he replied and said, "Yes, what is left of me." He said to the Capt., "If you had to have kept your whistle blowing, and your father had not ordered us overboard, this thing would never have happened."

George Tuff, Survivor

I am sure that had we the wireless aboard of her this spring this disaster would not have occurred. Our ship could have got in touch with the other steamers and they would have come to our assistance.

Abram Kean, Master of the *Stephano*

So far as risk is concerned, there is no man that goes to the seal fishery can possibly avoid taking risks; it is a risky voyage from the start to finish, and if any man makes up his mind that he is not going to take any risks, his only safe way is to stay at home.

First to the Rescue.

"I was the first of the Bellaventure's men to get out on the ice, when we found out that disaster had overtaken the Newfoundland's men," said A. Crowdy of Pouch Cove. "John Wall was with me and we discovered the first of the bodies.

"It was a terrible sight to behold. Men without any life in them lay sprawled about on the ice in all positions. Across one another and side by side they lay. Good God I hope never to see such a sight again."

Mr. Crowdy said that the first man he saw was an old chum of his and a native of Pouch Cove and he was absolutely lifeless.

"I went on further," he said, "and found a young fellow who was almost [illegible] I had to prise open his jaw

A rescuer from the *Bellaventure* speaks to the *Daily Mail* about his experiences on April 2, 1914. *Daily Mail, April 6, 1914*

Search parties look for survivors and bodies. *ASCD, Coll. 115 16.04.036 (top), Coll. 115 16.04.065 (bottom)*

Reaction

MR. COAKER'S LOG

April 3rd — Ice continued tightly packed. About 1 p.m. a little swell rolled in and opened the ice a little. The ships were given some freedom, and about 4 p.m. the weather cleared, disclosing the *Florizel*, *Newfoundland* and *Stephano* within a mile of us, while the *Beothic* and *Bellaventure* were a little further distant. The *Adventure* and *Bonaventure* were about five miles distant.

Sixty-nine bodies had been recovered and placed on board of the *Bellaventure*. Nothing further could be done. The *Bellaventure* soon started for home and got away a few miles owing to the slack in the floe. The *Newfoundland* did not appear to make any attempt to follow.

The *Beothic* being homeward bound of course endeavoured to follow the *Bellaventure*. Those on board [the *Nascopie*] who had near relatives on the *Newfoundland* are frantic with grief. All are grief stricken and don't want to handle any more seals this spring.

ANXIOUS INQUIRIES

Several came weeping anxious to learn of the fate of loved ones who sailed in the *Newfoundland*. We spoke to no ship after we reached the scene of the disaster. All we saw was carcasses of seals and numerous gulls. Strange some of the ships did not attempt to communicate verbally. What we know of the awful calamity is but little, although on the spot.

The men are asking hundreds of questions which can't be answered. What caused the men to be out is the universal question which I fear won't be answered until evidence before a court of enquiry reveals the facts.

Our men were out until about 1 p.m. on that fatal day, but no careful observant master would have allowed his men to scatter far from the ship on that day. Our men were picking up scattered seals, but none of them went far from the ship. When the first dwye of snow came on we had several men on the ice about half a mile from the ship. We lost sight of them while the dwye was on. It soon cleared again and they came on board.

UNCERTAIN WEATHER

Another dwye came on and lasted for, say, 15 minutes and again cleared up. This was followed by more snow which did not slacken for the evening and night. The day was one that threatened weather, although not over cold. The wind increased in velocity. The temperature fell lower and lower. Not much snow fell. The drift was sharp, cutting like a knife.

My opinion is that most of the men survived the first night (Tuesday). The first night's exposure coupled with the total absence of a warm stimulant left the men exhausted, and Wednesday's high wind, drift and bitter frost, was too much for human beings to overcome, and seeing no hope of rescue owing to the tight nature of the heavy Arctic floe, many laid down to die long before Wednesday's fearful night passed.

On Wednesday evening about 4 p.m. the sky cleared and had the other ships been notified of the disaster relief crews could have searched the floe before nightfall, although it was bitterly cold and a close drift swept over the floe.

ALL WAS COMFORT

On board the *Nascopie* all was comfort and contentment, and no one thought of any poor chap being astray on the broad ocean on such a night.

We steamed until nightfall and once more burned down. This is another stormy night. Snowing with a stiff breeze. Our ship's company is silent; few gather in groups and in whispers discuss what they know about the disaster.

The *Bellaventure* in St. John's harbour, ca. 1913-1915. The Newfoundland government ordered the *Bellaventure* to gather all *Newfoundland* survivors and bodies and bring them to St. John's. *MHA, PF-345.012*

Word of the disaster reached St. John's by telegraph on April 2 and soon spread across the island. The Newfoundland government called an emergency meeting to coordinate its response. It invited representatives from the merchant firms that owned the *Newfoundland* and *Bellaventure* to attend. How to receive the injured and dead sealers topped the agenda.

They ordered the *Bellaventure* to gather all the survivors and bodies and then return to St. John's as quickly as possible. A team of doctors and nurses stood by and the General Hospital's surgical ward was set aside to receive the most badly injured. In downtown St. John's, the King George V Seamen's Institute was converted into a temporary hospital for the other survivors. A morgue was also set up there and the government had 100 coffins made.

The immediate public reaction was one of shock and grief. Outrage would come later, when people began to question how merchant firms and government regulated the industry. But for now, there was only sorrow and concern for the sealers and their families. Business ground to a halt and cable offices were jammed with people desperate for news. Information came in slowly from the icefields but it was filled with gaps.

A temporary morgue was set up at the King George V Seamen's Institute in downtown St. John's. *ASCD, Coll. 115 16.04.049*

The Newfoundland government ordered 100 coffins made for the dead *Newfoundland* sealers. *ASCD, Coll. 115 16.04.084*

"How many men were out is at present unknown, nor is it known how many men managed to get back safe to the ship," the *Evening Telegram* reported on April 2. "All that is known is that the *Bellaventure* found fifty of them dead and dying on the ice." It printed a partial list of survivors the following day, alongside the first of many sympathy letters that poured in from the public. It also solicited donations to help victims and their families. The disaster fund totalled more than $88,500 by the end of the month.

Names of Those Who Succumbed to the Ravages of the Storm:

Thomas King, St. John's
David Locke, St. John's
Raymond Bastow, St. John's
Chas. Davis, St. John's
Chas. Olsen, St. John's
Daniel Downey, St. John's
Nick Morey, St. John's
Wm. J. Pear, Thorburn Road
Sam Squires, Topsail
Jas. Porter, Manuels
John Taylor, Long Pond
John Ryan, Goulds
Arthur Mullowney, Bay Bulls
Peter Gosse, Torbay
John Lawlor, Horse Cove
John Butler, Pouch Cove
Thos. Jordan, Pouch Cove
H. Jordan, Pouch Cove
Valentine Butler, Pouch Cove
Bernard Jordan, Pouch Cove
Geo. Leewhiting, Hr. Grace
John Brazil, Harbor Grace
Jos. Hiscock, Carbonear
Robt. Matthews, New Perlican
Chas. Warren, New Perlican
Hez. Seward, New Perlican
Peter Seward, New Perlican
Ed. Tippet, Catalina
Geo. Carpenter, Catalina
Abel Tippet, Catalina
Wm. J. Tippet, Catalina
Norman Tippet, Catalina
Wm. Fleming, Bonavista
Fred. Carroll, Bonavista
Thos. Hicks, Bonavista
Sim. Cuff, Bonavista
Benj. Chalk, Bonavista
Robt. Brown, Fair Island, B.B.
Jonas Pickett, Fair Island
Wm. Oldford, Elliston
Chas. Cole, Elliston
Albert J. Crew, Elliston
Noah Tucker, Elliston
Sam Martin, Elliston
Reuben Crew, Elliston
Alex. Goodland, Elliston
John Mercer, Bay Roberts
Jas. Bradbury, Bay Roberts
Ben. J. Marsh, Deer Isld., T.B.
Fred. Percy, Winterton, T.B.
Phil. Dohey, Placentia
Jno. Lundrigan, Red Island, P.B.
Jos. Williams, Ferryland
James Ryan, Fermeuse
Job Easton, Greenspond
Alan Warren, Han'ts Hr.
Michael Joy, Harbor Main
Albert Kelloway, Perrys Cove
Pat. Corbett, Clarke's Beach

And balance of men taken at Wesleyville who are not on the saved list.

A partial list of the dead.
Evening Telegram, April 4, 1914

At the ice floes, the steamers gathered to identify the dead. Wes Kean boarded the *Bellaventure* and was overwhelmed by a horrible scene. His men looked like eerie statues, frozen and terrible in lifelike positions. Some were kneeling, some were curled up on their sides, and a few seemed to be dancing. He saw the Tippett family, still standing together, and the Crewe father and son in their heartbreaking embrace. Walking among the bodies, he identified his crew.

When it was over, he had counted 69 bodies and 55 survivors. Eight men were never found: Henry Dowden, Philip Holloway, James Howell, Henry Jordan, David Locke, Ezra Melendy, Art Mouland, and Mike Murray. All of the survivors were transferred to the *Bellaventure*, except for George Tuff, Arthur Mouland, and Elias Mouland, who remained aboard the *Newfoundland* to help navigate the wooden-wall back home. It would take the *Bellaventure* a day and a half to

Bodies of the *Newfoundland* sealers on the deck of the *Bellaventure*.
MHA, PF-345.013

New York Pledges At Least $10,000

New York, April 9.—At last night's meeting at New York, $5,000 was pledged, and arrangements made for raising at least $10,000 for the relief fund.

Mayor Ellis was chairman, and ... Newfoundlanders were pres-

1-14-13-100M

D. R. R. 6.

Sent Date

MARCONI WIRELESS TELEGRAPH COMPANY OF AMERICA

27 WILLIAM STREET, (Lord's Court Building), NEW YORK

No. 1	STEPHANO STATION	April 2 1914
Prefix Msg 355 P	Words 31	
Office of Origin Bellaventure		
Service Instructions: Radio		

Station Rec'd from	Time Rec'd	By whom Rec'd
	m.	
Station Sent to	**Time Sent**	**By whom sent**
	4.00 p m.	

To: Capt. Randell Bellaventure

I think it would be good plan after we get all men picked up make for Newfoundland and get roll call to get extent of loss.

A Kean

Landing Survivors

MR. COAKER'S LOG

April 4th — Day fine and clear. Wind off shore. Ice very tight. Just as bad as yesterday morning. Ice opened a little at 2 p.m. *Newfoundland* and *Adventure* close by. *Florizel* and *Stephano* [a] few miles distant picking up pans. No seals. Men anxious to get the list of dead belonging to *Newfoundland*, but in vain. Crews of ships grief stricken and every sealer expected owners of steel ships would order them in, accompanying the *Bellaventure* as a mark of respect for the dead, but all waited in vain. It is not 77 dead bodies of sealers sacrificed for greed they are interested in, but seals, which apparently are of more interest to them.

MESSAGE AND ANSWER

Seeing no proper action taken I, on behalf of men, marconied the following message: "Job, St. John's.

"Crews fleet grief stricken. Prospects nil. Suggest owners recall steel fleet accompany *Bellaventure* St. John's respect dead."

This message was sent as soon as the operator obtained a chance this morning. The *Beothic* is reported as having arrived at noon.

At 4 p.m. the following message was received in reply to the one mentioned above:

"Coaker, *Nascopie*.

"Via Cape Race.

"Decision as to prospects getting more seals must be left entirely to the captain. Please don't interfere. JOB."

Such a ridiculous reply showed exactly what knowledge owners ashore have of the feelings of the sealers on the ocean, and how easily it is for them to deceive themselves as to what transpire on board the ships at sea.

IMPROFITABLE WORK

Anyone on the spot knows what the prospects are when a ship like the *Nascopie* takes 250 seals in a week and April the 4th is reached: when every harp pupped has taken to the water. But the object of the appeal, which was to have the 69 sealer bodies escorted to port in a national manner, compatible with the respect which the whole fleet considers was due to the memory of the 77 men who died in an endeavor to secure wealth to maintain their country, and whose lives were sacrificed to greed for gold.

Heartlessness in the extreme is the action of the owners of the steel ships in expecting men to mourn the loss of 77 comrades by scouring the seas in quest of more seals, while their loved ones were being outwardly mourned by strangers in port only 40 miles away, and to make the disrespect more pronounced, the *Beothic* should fly away at high pressure in order to secure the honor of being first ship to port, leaving the *Bellaventure* to creep along as she may with her 69 dead forms of human freight and 46 souls just rescued from the jaws of death.

A crowd of about 10,000 waits for the *Bellaventure* to arrive in St. John's. *ASCD, Coll. 115 16.04.045*

Hundreds of people lined the St. John's waterfront on April 4 to wait for the *Bellaventure*. Many had been there since dawn. All day long, newspaper offices and the Board of Trade posted updates in their windows of the vessel's slow progress toward land. Flags everywhere were at half-mast. So was the *Bellaventure*'s when it finally steamed through the Narrows at about 5 p.m.

It took doctors, nurses, and volunteers more than an hour to escort the survivors off the vessel. Some could still walk; others had to be carried off on stretchers. Almost everyone bore marks of frostbite—their necks, wrists, and hands badly swollen, their skin discoloured and covered in sores.

John Keels died on April 18, bringing the *Newfoundland* disaster's death toll to 78. He was 22 years old and married. Nine months passed before the final survivor was released from the General Hospital. Most recovered, but some had to have toes, fingers, or feet amputated.

The survivors endured psychological wounds too. "I was home a long time before I could sleep," Cecil Mouland later said. "I used to wake up in the night hollering and I could see men on the ice. I used to tell my mother, you know, I could see men on the pans of ice like they was coming up. It was just a dream, I suppose, and I'd wake up and holler."

The *Bellaventure* arrives at St. John's. *MHA, PF-055.2-F48*

After the survivors were taken to hospital, the 69 bodies were removed from the *Bellaventure*. The sight "sent a shudder through those who saw it," reported the *Evening Telegram* in a special edition released that night. "The bodies had been laid there just as they were brought in from the ice, many of them with limbs contracted and drawn up in all postures which the cold had brought about." Relatives and friends waited to receive their dead at the Seamen's Institute.

Recovered bodies stowed on the *Bellaventure*'s deck.
MHA, PF-345.014 (top); ASCD, Coll. 115 16.04.041 (bottom)

BELLAVENTURE REACHES PORT WITH SURVIVORS AND THE DEAD

MR. COAKER'S LOG

REGRETTABLE

The fame-seeking anxiety of the captain of the *Beothic* and the indifference of her owners for the feelings of the toiling masses of the Colony, whose sons and brothers had died as heroes upon the Arctic ice floes in pursuance of their calling, is to be greatly regretted, for the *Beothic* at least should have been ordered to closely accompany the *Bellaventure* to St. John's, and thus pay some reasonable respect to the many dead who through no fault of theirs had been called upon to sacrifice their lives up on the frozen floe, after enduring the most excruciating torture.

But even this small token of respect was denied our almost assassinated countrymen. They were only toilers was the innermost thought of the slave owners; let us take it quietly and the whole thing will blow over in a few days.

To the insulting reply above quoted was sent the following:

"Job, St. John's.

"Taken 250 past week. Exceedingly obliged advice tendered. COAKER."

LACK OF THOUGHT

Whoever penned the Job reply must have done so without consideration, for only an irresponsible could have imagined that I would interfere in any way to influence the captain or the crew under the circumstances.

I hear on all sides the desire of the crew to see the faces of the dead heroes and their hope that the owners would respect the dead by ordering the ships to port in funeral order as a national mark of respect for their dead comrades.

Eight bodies of the 77 deaths as a result of the disaster, not recovered.

The *Diana* came in sight at 6 p.m. and we steamed towards her in order to give her a supply of coal, which we succeeded in accomplishing. Had conversation with several of the *Diana*'s crew. They knew nothing of the disaster until they came alongside. Some of the men report a slight improvement in the food on board since we spoke to her on Thursday. The *Diana* finished coaling at night.

News of the disaster spread quickly. Survivors told their stories to reporters, and photographs of the dead and injured circulated widely. Even the *New York Times* ran a story. Donations to the relief fund poured in from all over the world. England's Royal Family gave money. So did the Queen of Denmark and the Canadian government. A local amateur theatre troupe presented the proceeds of its performances of the comedy *Pepita*, which played in St. John's from April 13 to April 18, 1914.

The impact of the tragedy on the Newfoundland public was intense and would have far-reaching implications. Letters flooded newspaper offices. Most expressed sympathy, but there was also a growing anger. People questioned how the industry treated its men. They wanted to know how such a tragedy could have happened.

Wealthy merchant firms

An ambulance waits for survivors of the *Newfoundland* disaster.
The Rooms Provincial Archives Division, VA 164-13

PAGES TO-DAY. THE "PEOPLE'S PAPER" IS A LIVE DAILY IN A BUSY CENTRE—STUDY ITS NEWSY ADVERTISING. TEN P

THE EVENING TELEGRAM.

PRICE ONE CENT. ST. JOHN'S, NEWFOUNDLAND, SATURDAY, APRIL 4, 1914. $3.00 PER YEAR.

The S.S. BELLAVENTURE

Arrives With the Dead

And Suffering Sealers--Heartrending Scenes as Ship Enters Port --- Wide-spread Sympathy With the Afflicted -- Arrangements for Public Funeral Being Considered.

Evening Telegram Special Edition, April 4, 1914

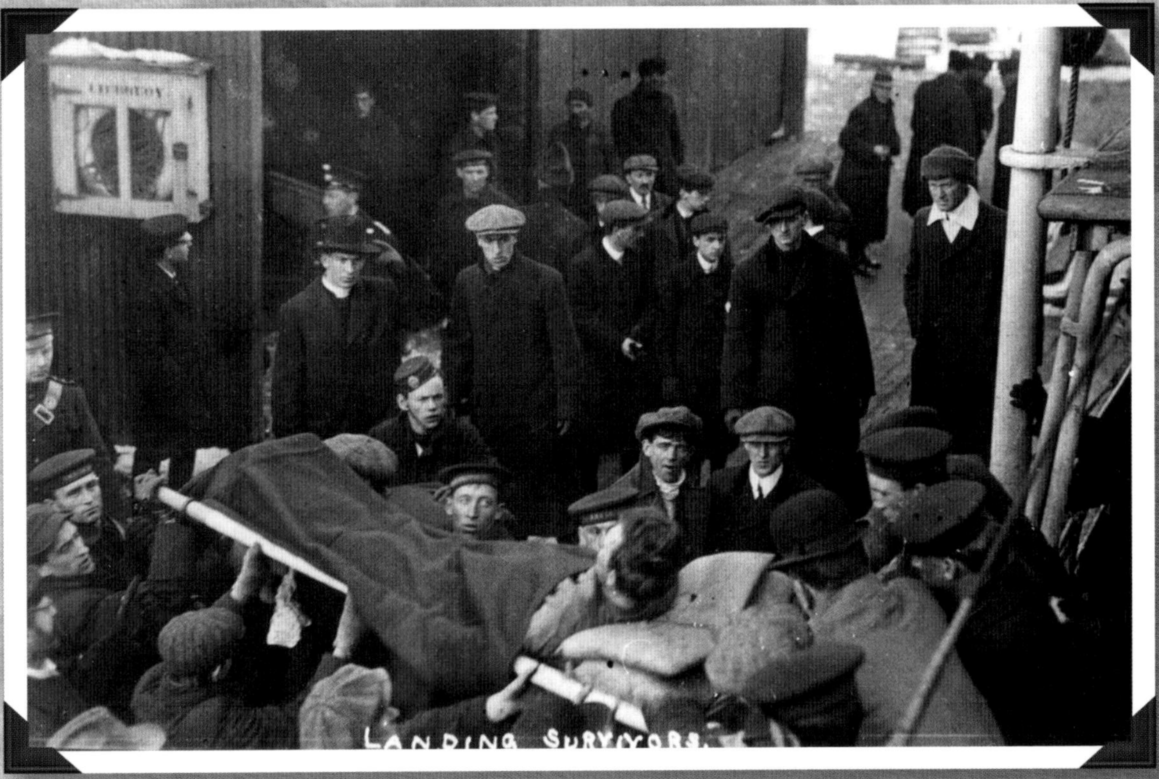

came under intense public scrutiny and so did the ice captains. On April 4, Coaker wrote of his disgust that the *Nascopie* continued hunting and that the *Beothic* was racing home with its load of pelts. A similar distaste was spreading throughout Newfoundland. Could profit warrant so much risk? It was time for a change.

The public pressured the government to act and it quickly established a Magisterial Enquiry into the *Newfoundland* disaster to determine if anyone was criminally responsible. Headed by Judge A.W. Knight, it would begin hearing testimony on April 7. Survivors, rescuers, and medical personnel would all testify. Even the ice captains and merchants would have to take the stand. Everything would be made public in local newspapers as it unfolded.

But first there was another priority. Families had to bury their dead. There were many funeral services in the coming days. Some were in St. John's, but as most of the men came from outport Newfoundland, their bodies were taken home for burial.

Landing survivors. *ASCD, Coll. 203 8.01.001 (top); The Rooms Provincial Archives Division VA 164-9 (bottom)*

Mourning and Mutiny

MR. COAKER'S LOG

SAW *SAGONA*

April 5th — Steamed 25 miles South in the early morning. Burnt down 50 miles East of Cape St. Francis. *Sagona* passed us in the afternoon; did not speak to her. Silent day on board.

Held memorial service at 7 p.m. consisting of Litany, Hymns, and the Burial Service. Addresses by Wesley Howell, Skipper Peter Gaulton, Wm. Hounsell, and myself, after which several prayed. It was a joint service by Churchmen and Methodists, and was exceedingly impressive. All the crew attended. It occupied nearly three hours. The Litany and Hymns seemed very appropriate. The Burial Service was splendidly read by Fred Tulk, of Newtown; Wesley Howell, of Cat Harbor, reading the lesson. Many an eye was wet with tears. Skipper Peter Gaulton spoke very feelingly of his experience at the time of the *Greenland* disaster, he being one of the crew on that voyage. Probably 50 of our present crew were on board of the *Greenland* that spring.

MEMORIAL SERVICE

Those present at the memorial service will long remember it. Those heartless lovers of gold ashore so indifferent to the feelings of the toilers respecting the *Newfoundland* disaster should learn a thing or two from the manner in which the *Nascopie*'s crew respected the memory of their dead comrades tonight. Very few of the *Nascopie*'s crew will waste much time in considering how much respect the shipowners at St. John's have for those who risk their lives from year to year in order to maintain their country, their homes and maintain in luxury those who reap the cream of the seal fishery.

Members of the St. John's Ambulance Association who responded to the *Newfoundland* disaster. The association was founded in 1910 to provide first aid in emergency situations. *City of St. John's Archives, 1.35.001*

MHA, PF-318.030

The sudden loss of so many lives had devastating effects in Newfoundland. Parents grieved for their sons and children were left fatherless. Widows had to deal with their sorrow and the added burden of making ends meet without a breadwinner. The small and tightly knit communities that the men came from were demoralized and economically shaken. Eight of the victims were from Elliston—a huge loss for a settlement of about 850 people.

People unconnected to the disaster also mourned. Day after day, local newspapers published dozens of sympathy notes and donations poured in to the relief fund, which totalled $300,000 by August. In St. John's, thousands of people accompanied a funeral procession on April 5, as horse-drawn sleighs carried the dead to the train station so they could be returned home for burial. Memorial services were held across the island and even at sea, on the *Nascopie* and many of the other steamers still at the icefields. The disaster had seeped into the Newfoundland psyche.

Anger soon mingled with grief. On land, newspaper columns and letters to the editor criticized the merchant firms and ice captains for placing the sealers at such tremendous risk. "[T]he question rises whether Captain Abram Kean is to be held morally responsible for the great loss of life among the men sent out by the *Newfoundland*," the *Evening Telegram* editorialized on April 6. People waited anxiously for the enquiry to begin the following day.

Still at sea, Abram Kean was being chal-

Nº ....

In replying the number & date of this letter should be quoted.

General Hospital,
St. John's, Newfoundland,

DECEMBER 21ST. 4. 191

LIST OF SEALERS FROM "S. S. NEWFOUNDLAND".

STANLEY	ANDREWS.	NEWTOWN.	FROSTBURN FEET & FACE.
HEDLEY	PAYN.	GREENSPOND.	.. TOES & SNOWBLINDNESS.
CECIL	MOULAND.	DOTING COVE.	SLIGHT FROSTBURN FEET.
HENRY	KELLOWAY.	PERRYS COVE.	.. .. TOES & EARS.
JOSHUA	HOLLOWAY.	NEW HARBOR,	.. .. TOES & FINGERS
JOHN	FISHER.	BONAVISTA.	.. .. TOES. SNOW BLINDNESS
~~THOMAS~~	~~SHEPPARD~~.	~~CATALINA~~.	~~PNEUMONIA~~.
GEORGE	TREMLETT.	BONAVISTA.	SLIGHT FROSTBURN GREAT TOES. SNOW BLINDNESS.
WILLIAM	CUFF.	DOTING COVE.	SLIGHT FROSTBURN GREAT TOES.
HUGH	MOULAND.	BONAVISTA.	SLIGHT FROSTBURN GREAT & LITTLE

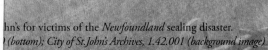

...hn's for victims of the *Newfoundland* sealing disaster.
...) (bottom); City of St. John's Archives, 1.42.001 (background image)

Southern Cross Disaster

While the *Newfoundland*'s men were stranded on the North Atlantic ice floes, a second tragedy had been unfolding farther south, one that resulted in an even greater loss of life. The *Southern Cross* had spent the spring in the Gulf of St. Lawrence. The hunting was good and by March 26 there were 18,000 pelts on board—a sizeable cargo for the small wooden steamer. Captain George Clarke decided it was time to head home.

The vessel was riding low in the water and tilting to one side under its heavy load, but that was not unusual for a return voyage. The ice captains and merchants pushed their steamers as hard as they did their sealers. There was no punishment for overloading a ship, but there were many rewards for bringing back as large a cargo as possible. Clarke knew that he stood a good chance of being the first ice master home that spring, an honour the captains annually vied for.

Baine Johnston and Company supplied the *Southern Cross*, but the merchant firm had not installed any wireless equipment on board. As a result, the vessel's return trip and ultimate disappearance can only be reconstructed through second-hand information: visual sightings and wireless messages sent by other vessels or telegraph stations. There are few. On March 30, a telegraph officer at St. Pierre reported that a black steamer with three masts and a yellow funnel had passed out of the Gulf. That description could only belong to the *Southern Cross*.

MR. COAKER'S LOG

April 6th — Fine day, wind moderate. Steamed all day towards the inside water, but found ice packed and made no progress. Took 11 seals. Saw *Stephano*, *Florizel*, *Newfoundland*. *Adventure* reports the loss of two and a half blades of her propellor. Had ticket lottery for 3 empty pork barrels. Winner Skipper Darius Hall, Hr. Keefe and George Ivany. Winners had to boil a gallon of molasses into "bullseyes" [a hard candy]. They started at 9 p.m. and did not finish until 4 a.m. next morning. They well earned their barrels.

UNEASINESS

No word of the *Southern Cross* all day; is causing much uneasiness on board, but the general opinion is that she is safe although driven to sea.

Everyone is asking why a ship costing $250 a day is kept out to take 11 seals, probably worth $15; but of course the wiseacres ashore know best concerning such matters. Burnt down at 8 p.m. in heavy ice. Snowing a part of the night with strong North wind.

The *Southern Cross* in St. John's harbour, ca. 1910. *City of St. John's Archives, 7.05.011*

THE DAILY MAIL.

"BLOODHOUND" REACHES PORT; AND REPORTS HAVING SIGHTED QUANTITY OF WRECKAGE AFLOAT

TO CONTINUE | MUST HAVE COME | OF UNFORTUNATE

The wreckage that the *Bloodhound* reported was later discovered to be wood from a wharf and a biscuit box. *Daily Mail, April 13, 1914*

Sealers try to pull the *Southern Cross* free of pack ice in St. John's harbour, n.d. *ASCD, Coll. 115 16.04.003*

Vessel Profile: *Southern Cross*
The *Southern Cross* was an old and storied vessel. Built at Arendal, Norway, in 1886, the wooden steamer had taken the Anglo-Norwegian polar explorer Carsten Borchgrevink to Antarctica in 1898. During that voyage, it became one of the first vessels to break through the Great Ice barrier and explore the Ross Sea. Following Borchgrevink's return home in June 1900, he was honoured by the American Geographical Society and knighted by Sweden's King Oscar II. The *Southern Cross* was sent to Newfoundland, where it took part in every seal hunt from 1901 until it was lost in 1914.

Then, shortly before noon on March 31, the mail boat *Portia* sighted the *Southern Cross* near Cape Pine, on the Avalon Peninsula's south coast. The *Portia* was heading for the nearby port of St. Mary's Bay to wait out the worsening storm—the same storm that would soon strand the *Newfoundland*'s men—but it looked as if the *Southern Cross* was heading farther east, perhaps for Cape Race. If so, it was a dangerous decision. The vessel would have to contend with gale-force winds, rough seas, and thick snow that had reduced visibility to almost zero. Compounding this was the problem of Freels Rock. Submerged in just 3 fathoms (about 5.5 metres) of water, it was a hazard to any passing vessel. The *Southern Cross* exchanged whistle calls with the *Portia*, and was never seen again.

Many people in Newfoundland were initially optimistic that the *Southern Cross* would soon turn up in St. John's or another port. It was not unusual for a vessel to stop communication, especially if it didn't have wireless, or to arrive late at a port. "The general opinion is that she was driven off to sea and will not be heard from for a couple of days," the *Evening Telegram* reported on April 2. By then, word of the *Newfoundland* disaster had reached land, and it was unthinkable that there could be more loss of life.

Concern steadily grew. On April 3, the Newfoundland government asked the *Seneca*, a U.S. patrol ship operating in the area, to report any sightings of the *Southern Cross*. It also dispatched the *Kyle*, a local coastal steamer, to search for the missing vessel. Other ships joined the effort in the coming days but could not find any concrete sign of the *Southern Cross* or its crew.

The *Kyle* gave up its search on April 19, and the *Southern Cross* was presumed lost at sea with all hands. In January 1915, a battered chest carrying lifebelts washed up on Coll Island, west of Scotland. It was the first and only piece of wreckage positively identified as belonging to the *Southern Cross*.

The *Southern Cross* was carrying 173 men and one stowaway when it sank. It was the greatest loss of life in the seal hunt's history. When added to the 78 men who had died in the *Newfoundland* disaster, and to the death of Henry Pridham aboard the *Bonaventure* on March 22, the number of fatalities that spring totalled 253. On August 4, 1914, the *Evening Telegram* reported that the dead sealers from both the *Newfoundland* and *Southern Cross* disasters had left behind 721 dependants, which included 383 children.

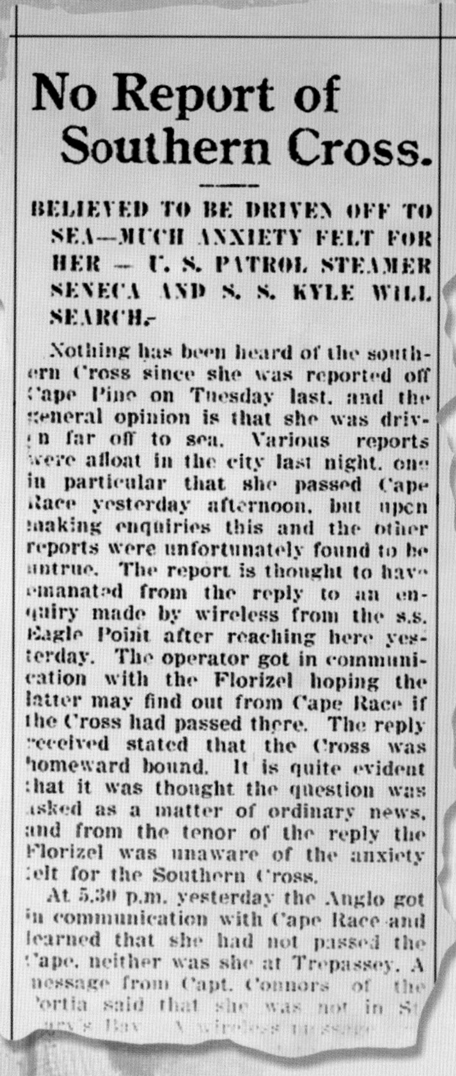

No Report of Southern Cross.

BELIEVED TO BE DRIVEN OFF TO SEA—MUCH ANXIETY FELT FOR HER — U. S. PATROL STEAMER SENECA AND S. S. KYLE WILL SEARCH.-

Nothing has been heard of the southern Cross since she was reported off Cape Pine on Tuesday last, and the general opinion is that she was driven far off to sea. Various reports were afloat in the city last night, one in particular that she passed Cape Race yesterday afternoon, but upon making enquiries this and the other reports were unfortunately found to be untrue. The report is thought to have emanated from the reply to an enquiry made by wireless from the s.s. Eagle Point after reaching here yesterday. The operator got in communication with the Florizel hoping the latter may find out from Cape Race if the Cross had passed there. The reply received stated that the Cross was homeward bound. It is quite evident that it was thought the question was asked as a matter of ordinary news, and from the tenor of the reply the Florizel was unaware of the anxiety felt for the Southern Cross.

At 5.30 p.m. yesterday the Anglo got in communication with Cape Race and learned that she had not passed the Cape, neither was she at Trepassey. A message from Capt. Connors of the Portia said that she was not in St. [illegible]

Evening Telegram, April 3, 1914

MOURNING THE *SOUTHERN CROSS*

MR. COAKER'S LOG

April 7th — Wind North, strong. Did not steam much in the forenoon. Men busy consuming "bullseyes." A report current concerning trouble amongst *Eagle's* crew in reference to taking coal from the *Florizel*. Not surprised in view of the feeling pervading the whole fleet since the disaster of April 1st. A hard feeling existed on board of the *Diana* when we were coaling her on Saturday. She has a few tough chaps on board and it would not surprise me to learn later that the captain had lots of trouble with some of the men.

Several of the *Diana's* crew left her on Saturday and are on board of the *Nascopie*. One man with an injured arm, named Gardner, was also sent on board of our ship for medical treatment. We have also a stowaway named Noftall, belonging to the *Diana*. Took 21 seals today. Cape St. Francis and Cape Spear quite visible to the naked eye from the deck, Signal Hill from the barrel. We are south of Cape Spear. *Sagona* in sight all the evening.

Still no word of the *Southern Cross* reported. Not a word received from the shore concerning the victims of the *Newfoundland* disaster. It was no trouble to know how many seals the Gulf ships had taken, but there was money in seals, when ships were loaded, which is of far more importance than the death and burial of 69 sealers.

Reported owners refused our captain permissions to give up the useless and costly quest for 20 seals per day, which strikes all as very singular, for few can understand why $300 is spent to secure $10 worth of seals; but like many other puzzlers, it will not be solved by the simple-minded toiler. I fancy I have a fair idea for the reasons for such inexplicable proceedings.

The night was beautifully clear and the moon shone in all its glory. The ocean was spotlessly white and a sight worth seeing. The *Sagona's* lights about one mile distant broke the isolation and monotony of spending night after night either without a ship in sight, or if in sight invisible through a heavy mist or snow or storm.

The disappearance of the *Southern Cross* remained unexplained. People in Newfoundland struggled to find closure, but they had no bodies to bury or tangible evidence that their loved ones had died.

Songs became a part of the mourning process because they could offer solace and explanation. One (pictured at right) expressed a hope that the lost men would eventually arrive home, but then concluded that they are likely in "that heavenly land … where cares and sorrow are no more, but all is peace and joy." The disaster was part of God's plan, according to the anonymous songwriter: "All things do happen for the best."

People scoured Newfoundland's inshore waters for any sign of the lost vessel. Long after the *Kyle* abandoned its search on April 19, rumoured sightings of wreckage persisted. Some, including an anonymous letter written to the *Evening Telegram* on June 19, said they did more harm than good: "Sorrow is being continuously renewed when we hear of these false reports of certain wreckage being picked up, which is supposed to be that of the *Southern Cross*. For years to come the memory of that terrible disaster will be fresh in the minds of people."

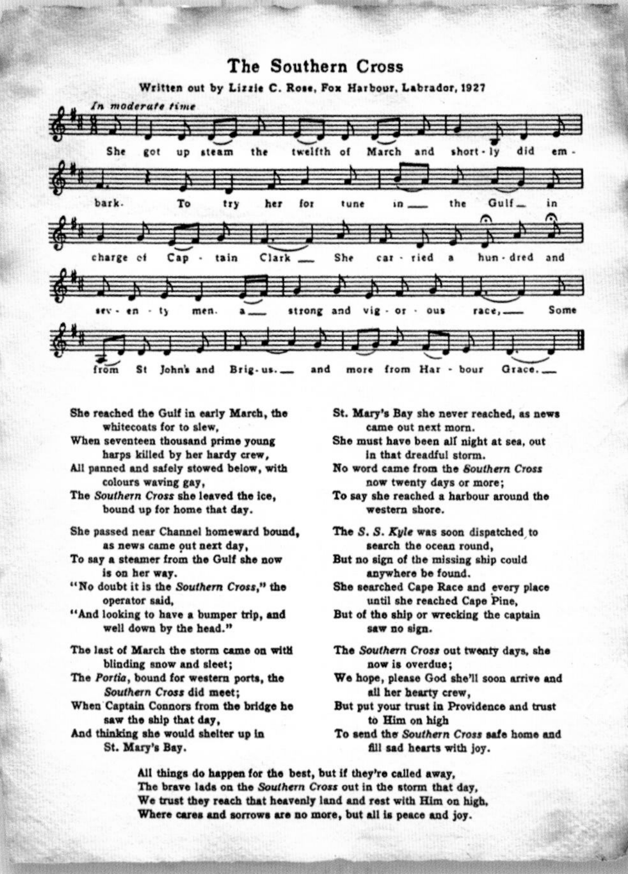
The Southern Cross

Written out by Lizzie C. Rose, Fox Harbour, Labrador, 1927

In moderate time
She got up steam the twelfth of March and short-ly did em-bark. To try her for tune in the Gulf in charge of Cap-tain Clark She car-ried a hun-dred and sev-en-ty men. a strong and vig-or-ous race, Some from St John's and Brig-us. and more from Har-bour Grace.

She reached the Gulf in early March, the whitecoats for to slew,
When seventeen thousand prime young harps killed by her hardy crew,
All panned and safely stowed below, with colours waving gay,
The *Southern Cross* she leaved the ice, bound up for home that day.

She passed near Channel homeward bound, as news came out next day,
To say a steamer from the Gulf she now is on her way.
"No doubt it is the *Southern Cross*," the operator said,
"And looking to have a bumper trip, and well down by the head."

The last of March the storm came on with blinding snow and sleet;
The *Portia*, bound for western ports, the *Southern Cross* did meet;
When Captain Connors from the bridge he saw the ship that day,
And thinking she would shelter up in St. Mary's Bay.

St. Mary's Bay she never reached, as news came out next morn.
She must have been all night at sea, out in that dreadful storm.
No word came from the *Southern Cross* now twenty days or more;
To say she reached a harbour around the western shore.

The *S. S. Kyle* was soon dispatched to search the ocean round,
But no sign of the missing ship could anywhere be found.
She searched Cape Race and every place until she reached Cape Pine,
But of the ship or wrecking the captain saw no sign.

The *Southern Cross* out twenty days, she now is overdue;
We hope, please God she'll soon arrive and all her hearty crew,
But put your trust in Providence and trust to Him on high
To send the *Southern Cross* safe home and fill sad hearts with joy.

All things do happen for the best, but if they're called away,
The brave lads on the *Southern Cross* out in the storm that day,
We trust they reach that heavenly land and rest with Him on high,
Where cares and sorrows are no more, but all is peace and joy.

From *Old Time Songs and Poetry of Newfoundland*, by Gerald S. Doyle, 1927.

S. H. PARSONS & SONS

When I heard that the *Southern Cross* last spring had the load of seals which she was reported to have had, and observing the storm on the 31st of March, I did not have any hope that she would come through it if she met the storm off Cape Pine. When I heard the report of the *Portia* having seen her near Cape Pine, I knew she was in a bad situation.
—*Testimony from John Clarke, a former captain of the* Southern Cross *and brother of the late Captain George Clarke*

The *Southern Cross* docked at St. John's harbour (second vessel from the right). *City of St. John's Archives, 7.05.033*

The government established a Marine Court of Enquiry to investigate the loss of the *Southern Cross*. It was led by Judge A.W. Knight, who also conducted the Magisterial Enquiry into the *Newfoundland* disaster. Witnesses included sealing captains, the vessel's managing owner (the merchant Walter Baine Grieve), and crewmembers of vessels that had sighted the *Southern Cross* either in the Gulf of St. Lawrence or on its voyage home.

Several theories were advanced to explain its disappearance, but the storm and a heavy cargo were the most widely accepted. In his final report, Knight wrote: "There is no direct evidence as to the cause of her loss, but I am of the opinion she foundered and went down with all hands in the heavy gale and snowstorm on the 31st in [the] vicinity of Freels Rock, which lies two miles offshore W. 1/2S. from Cape Pine."

The *Southern Cross* disaster brought about legislative change. In 1916, the government required all steamers to be marked with load lines. The owner of any vessel that returned to port with its load line below the water could be fined up to $2,500. Lifeboats became mandatory on steamers as did annual inspections.

From the final report of the search vessel *Kyle*
We saw nothing to give any indication of any wreckage until the 15th at 7 p.m. It had been very very foggy all day and we were steaming about four knots per hour, when a white coat pelt was sighted near the ship on the port bow. A few minutes afterwards another pelt was seen on the starboard bow. The mate, who had the bridge at the time, reports that at some time previous he had seen several spots of grease on the water. This was in the region of what is known as the gully between the Green Bank and the Great Bank, I might say this [is] in a direct drift from Cape Pine. All that could be possibly done in cruising for the steamer has been done. Lookout was kept night and day.

The SS *Kyle*, which searched for the *Southern Cross* from April 4 to 19, 1914. *MHA, PF-055.2-N66*

A Call for Change

MR. COAKER'S LOG

April 8th — Splendid day. *Sagona* came alongside. Had not heard of the *Newfoundland* disaster or the disappearance of the *Southern Cross*. Some of the *Sagona*'s crew reported food conditions to be extremely unsatisfactory. Bread unfit for food. No fresh beef, no brewse. Beans three times for the trip. No potatoes or turnips. Nothing for the pot. Even some cabin supplies short for some time.

We took about 20 seals. Passed North from 20 miles East of Cape Spear to about 25 miles East of Bonavista and returned.

The cook took a list of men approving of food supplied this voyage and all willingly gave their names. The only complaint possible being a shortage in the supply of fresh beef, which must be the result of an overlook. The cooks on the whole are well qualified for the work and would make good chefs if any ship required such an officer.

GOOD OFFICER

The chief cook, Samuel Tiller, who is known as the commodore, is indeed an attentive and efficient official and where he is in charge satisfaction must result.

The master watches are Kenneth Barbour, Ef. Barbour, sons of the late Capt. Wm. Barbour; Darius Hall and Walter Barbour, efficient and intelligent, as are also the assistant master watches, Isaac Squires, Robt. Barbour, Thos. Parsons, and Martin Curtis. The bridgemen are C. Barbour, John Collins, Alfred Gaulton, and J. Gushue. The quarter masters are Charles Tuff, Levi Green, David Rodgers, and James Davis. The wheelsmen Edgar Parsons, William Green, Sam. Edward, and Edward Perry. F. Newbury is the boatswain and Sm. Joliffe is his able mate. Thos. Perry is Carpenter. The captain's son, Pearce, is second in command and barrelman; Skipper Peter Gaulton second barrelman.

EXCELLENT CREW

There never was a crew more efficient or able than the crew of the *Nascopie*. Almost every sealer on board being a picked man.

The assistant cooks are Chas. Mullen, George Hayter, Robt. Fermage, Saml. Rodgers, Fred Tulk, baker, cabin cook, Martin Tulk; Wm. Grills, chief steward; captain's steward, Eli Hall; the mess room steward, Robt. Emerson.

The engineers are J. Ledinghom, John Black, Chesley Bond, and John Curran.

From my observations closely taken, I am of the opinion that every captain closely watches the movements and actions of Captain Abraham [Abram] Kean. I don't believe any captain is content when he is not in a position to know or judge what Capt. Abram is doing. I state this not because I have any kindly feelings towards Capt. Abram, but because I wish to give all concerned in this narrative their proper due.

PUSHING MAN

Capt. Wm. Winsor is a pushing young man and will, if he lives, become one of the foremost and most successful of our sealing masters. He has plenty of push and his judgement of seals is sound. His one fault being a careless disregard of his men when taking seals and his devil-daring in cutting off other crews. He came close to cutting down a pan of ice containing some of our crew while pelting seals. Some of them had to leave off pelting and run.

Captain George Barbour is a very steady commander, always cool and collected, and very careful over his men. They all respect him.

Capt. Bob Randell,
of "Bellaventure"
who had his master's
ticket at 21 yrs.

Captain Robert Randell of the *Bellaventure* was the first person to testify at the Magisterial Enquiry into the *Newfoundland* disaster on April 7, 1914. *The Rooms Provincial Archives Division, VA 164-4*

The 1914 sealing disasters placed the industry under intense public scrutiny. Merchants and ice captains watched their once unassailable power erode as newspapers, labour leaders, and the population in general began to hold them accountable for the safety of the sealing crews. Government fell under criticism for its lax regulations.

Day after day, newspapers published the proceedings of the Magisterial Enquiry into the *Newfoundland* disaster. Testimony was heard from many of the survivors and from the captains of the *Newfoundland*, *Stephano*, *Bellaventure*, and *Florizel*.

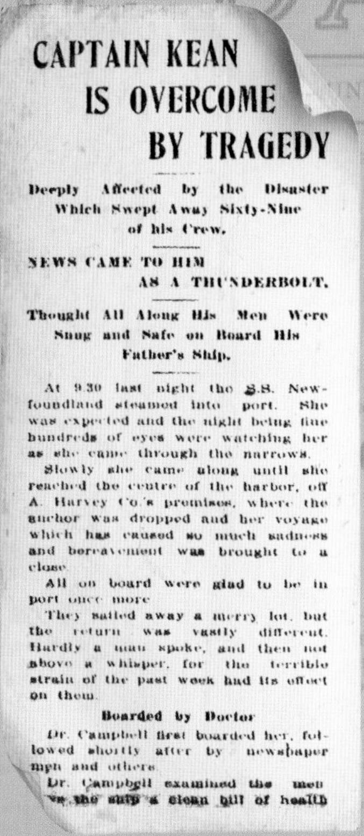

CAPTAIN KEAN IS OVERCOME BY TRAGEDY

Deeply Affected by the Disaster Which Swept Away Sixty-Nine of his Crew.

NEWS CAME TO HIM AS A THUNDERBOLT.

Thought All Along His Men Were Snug and Safe on Board His Father's Ship.

At 9.30 last night the S.S. Newfoundland steamed into port. She was expected and the night being fine hundreds of eyes were watching her as she came through the narrows.

Slowly she came along until she reached the centre of the harbor, off A. Harvey Co.'s premises, where the anchor was dropped and her voyage which has caused so much sadness and bereavement was brought to a close.

All on board were glad to be in port once more.

They sailed away a merry lot, but the return was vastly different. Hardly a man spoke, and then not above a whisper, for the terrible strain of the past week had its effect on them.

Boarded by Doctor

Dr. Campbell first boarded her, followed shortly after by newspaper men and others.

Dr. Campbell examined the men ve the ship a clean bill of health

Daily Mail, April 8, 1914

The survivors' stories were harrowing, heartbreaking, and often heroic. Some blamed Captain Abram Kean for ordering them off the *Stephano*, others pointed a finger at Westbury Kean, and a few criticized George Tuff. Some of the men simply accepted the ordeal as unavoidable—just part of a dangerous industry. The merchant firm of Harvey and Company also came under fire for removing the *Newfoundland*'s telegraph equipment. It was almost universally agreed by the captains and sealers alike that wireless would have averted the disaster.

As the enquiry proceeded, people learned about the nature of the seal hunt and of the men who took part in it. Practices previously taken for granted were now being questioned.

Survivor Ralph Mouland being carried off the *Bellaventure* on April 4, 1914. *ASCD, Coll. 115 16.04.047*

Why didn't all sealing steamers carry wireless equipment? Why should men work so far from their vessels? Why did they have to stay out on the ice after dark?

A picture of greedy merchants and power-hungry ice captains accumulating wealth by ignoring the sealers' safety emerged. Newspaper headlines and letters to the editor called for change. Abram Kean bore the brunt of the blame. His decision to continue sealing on April 4, followed by his unrepentant attitude at the enquiries, only fanned the public's anger. Westbury Kean, on the other hand, received far less negative attention. Filled with remorse and sorrow, he seemed a figure to be pitied instead of condemned.

Sustained public pressure brought about a shift in political will. The first significant change came in late 1914, when the legislature passed an Act requiring all steamers to carry wireless telegraph equipment. More laws and regulations would follow in the next two years.

The Directors Room of the merchant firm Job Brothers and Company, 1909. *MHA, PF-315.071*

Coaker's Campaign

MR. COAKER'S LOG

April 9th — Wind S.W., dull. About 20 miles from land. Took 26 beaters. Preparing for port. Decks washed. Ropes and gaffs given up. Captain, doctor, chief engineer, operator, Bryant, and myself lunched with Commodore Tiller in the cooks' quarters.

All seemed pleased to know ship heading for port. Officer gave a live seal a swim in a dory which they apparently much appreciated. We have one young hood and two small harp seals.

NOT CREDITABLE

The food supplied to the wooden ships is far from creditable to the owners, who of course will endeavor to escape the consequences of their negligence by asserting that the sealing law was not passed when the wooden ships sailed.

Such a defence will but reflect upon that useless blocking ornament of the Legislature—the Upper House—who kept the bill in slings for two weeks and succeeded in making it anything but a workable Act by the senseless and stupid amendments, most of which emanated from men whose only claim to a seat in that chamber consisted of their ability to personally abuse almost every decent man that took a part in public life for the last 30 years.

RESPONSIBLE PARTIES

The sealers in the wooden ships can thank the few swollen heads of the House of Lords for the conditions prevailing on the ships today. What is still worse is that those ships belong—except in the case of the *Fogota* and *Sagona*—to owners who three years ago signed an agreement binding themselves to put into operation most of the regulations which the Bill contained when it passed the House of Assembly.

Was Crosbie [John Chalker Crosbie, politician and businessman] right when he charged them in the House with having signed an agreement they did not intend to fulfill—it really looks as if they regard their honor as Morris does $380,000 a mere flea bite?

Conditions on board of the *Newfoundland*, *Fogota*, *Sagona*, *Eagle*, *Diana*, *Bloodhound*, *Ranger*, *Adventure*, and *Bellaventure* are far from what the law now require, and in some cases an outrage upon the common sense of the crews and a severe reflection upon the owners of such ships. Nothing like satisfaction is now afforded except on one or two ships.

FLEET MUST BE KEPT UP

There will be a stronger and far more better fight waged against those conditions during the next twelve months than has yet been experienced for the simple reason that we have now discovered that some of the owners have deliberately attempted to cod and fool the people by pretending to do what they had solemnly agreed to do three years ago, and which binds their honor as businessmen and respectable citizens. Nothing can excuse the conditions existing on the *Diana*, *Eagle*, *Fogota*, and *Sagona*—nothing but pure bluff. Almost every amendment made by the Legislative Council in the Coaker Sealing Bill has crippled the Bill, and will have to be rescinded.

The interests of a few sealing captains is not the interest of 4,000 sealers. The interest of three or four shipowners is not what will best preserve the interest of the Colony, and the amendment of the so-called Upper House had no object but to serve the interests of the owners and captains.

William F. Coaker, ca. 1930.
Newfoundland and Labrador Heritage Website

William Coaker emerged as one of the most vocal and effective advocates of sealers' rights. His speeches in the House of Assembly and frequent editorials in the *Daily Mail* invariably censured merchant firms and government officials for allowing the sealers to work under unnecessarily dangerous conditions.

In one letter, published on April 11, 1914, he called the disasters "the price of negligence and indifference," and asked, "What about the *Southern Cross*? Was she a fit and proper ship to clear for such a perilous voyage as seal hunting? Who will dare to say she was? Have not the insurance agencies refused to insure the *Newfoundland* for the past three springs?" He frequently called the sealing steamers "floating coffins."

Coaker was also dissatisfied with the Magisterial Enquiry into the *Newfoundland* disaster and the Marine Court of Enquiry into the disappearance of the *Southern Cross*. They were simply mandated to determine criminal liability in the case of the *Newfoundland* disaster (none was found) and suggest reasons for the sinking of the *Southern Cross* (overloading and stormy seas were likely to blame, but the absence of regular inspections also cast doubt on the vessel's seaworthiness).

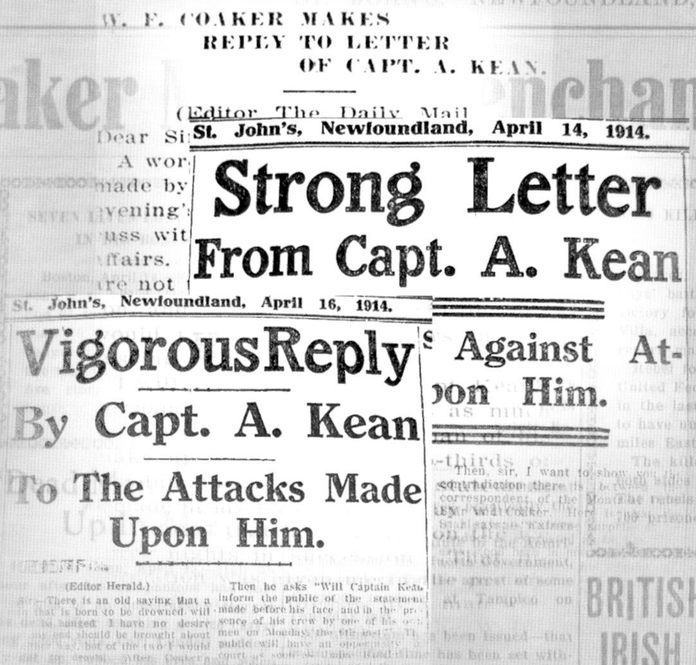

W. F. COAKER MAKES REPLY TO LETTER OF CAPT. A. KEAN.

St. John's, Newfoundland, April 14, 1914.

Strong Letter From Capt. A. Kean

St. John's, Newfoundland, April 16, 1914.

Vigorous Reply By Capt. A. Kean To The Attacks Made Upon Him.

Evening Herald, April 14 and April 16, 1914; Daily Mail, April, 15, 1914

Coaker questioned the *Southern Cross*'s seaworthiness, but the merchant Walter Baine Grieve testified at the Marine Court of Enquiry that it had been inspected just before the 1914 hunt. *MHA, PF-001.1-X12*

Coaker vs. Kean

Some of Coaker's most aggressive criticism was directed at Abram Kean. He wanted to know how a sealing captain with decades of experience could have left 132 men on the North Atlantic ice floes miles from their vessel and in a gathering storm. "While Newfoundland remains Captain Kean will be known as the man that could have averted the massacre of 77 of his countrymen but failed because he refused to make the effort," Coaker wrote in the *Daily Mail* on April 17, 1914.

Kean defended himself in letters to the *Evening Herald*. He said that he mistakenly thought the *Newfoundland* was only a two-hour walk away when he ordered the men off his vessel and that the barometer had not predicted a storm. He also accused Coaker of using the disaster for political leverage. By attacking Kean, a Conservative and a wealthy ice captain, Coaker stood to gain votes from the rural workers he and the Union Party strove to represent—sealers, fishers, and loggers.

Captain Abram Kean, ca. 1930s. *MHA, PF-118.001*

The two men waged a protracted public dispute. Coaker demanded that Kean be forever banned from the seal hunt and brought up on criminal charges. His petition to have Kean arrested collected thousands of signatures. But neither of the enquiries found Kean criminally liable and he never went to trial. In contrast, a jury ordered Coaker to pay Kean $500 for libel on March 11, 1915.

Coaker wanted to bring about more lasting change. He called upon the government to establish a Commission of Enquiry and empower it not only to investigate the disasters but also to recommend ways for legislators to make the seal hunt safer. His demands received widespread public support and, on April 25, the Newfoundland government announced that it would establish the enquiry and appoint three Supreme Court judges to lead it. Their report was due in February 1915 and would be made public not long after.

Commission of Enquiry

MR. COAKER'S LOG

ONLY JUST BEGUN

The work of protecting the interests of the people has but begun, and those who have used their well bought seats in the Legislative Council to block and nullify legislation on behalf of the Toilers [the working-class people Coaker strove to represent] will find that in future the Toilers will not be as reasonable and conciliatory as they have been. The supporters of the Government in the House did the knifing in both cases the past session of the Legislature, and Sir Edward Morris is blamed by many for having supported in the House what he could not oppose without bringing upon his head the contempt of the people; but although supporting them in the House he did very little to aid their passage through the Upper House.

Why Mr. [Augustus Frederick] Goodridge, one of Morris's recent appointments to the Legislative Council, actually moved to have the Sealing Bill shelved and submitted to the Select Committee which was considering some fishery matters. That should be an eye-opener to the Toilers. The double dealing of those political highwaymen will in future be exposed, because the Toilers now possess their own papers, and are consequently in a position to fight their enemies.

WILL NOT SUPPORT THEM

Not a single Union vote will be cast for a candidate that is not pledged to the abolition of the Legislative Council, and for this decision the Honourables of the Upper House can blame none but themselves. Sir Edward Morris has brought that Chamber into contempt by the manner in which he has stuffed it, and by using it as a blocking instrument to guillotine the decisions of the electorate, for the appointment of two political undesirables like Sidney Blandford and R.A. Squires, who were ousted from their seats in the People's House by majorities of 1,900 and 1,000 respectively, is about as hard a blow that any man could strike at the constitution of the Colony.

That two men could be found shamefaced enough to accept positions as Executive members and heads of departments, after being ignominiously turned down by their constituents, is something reasonable men cannot comprehend. That it stinks in the nostrils of the whole electorate is beyond doubt. That it was the only course that could be adopted to keep a minority government whose death warrant had been long since issued, in power in defiance of the electorate and the constitution no one now disputes.

SHOULD BE IMPEACHED

Governor Davidson should be impeached for allowing such an outrage to be perpetrated in a free country. His actions has called down upon his head the contempt of all right thinking people and few will now deny that Morris has no better friend or supporter in the Colony than the Governor.

Never again will Union members of the House of Assembly call upon him or pay him their respects. He allowed Morris to scorn the Legislature while it was in session the past winter in keeping those two positions vacant, in spite of the strong protest of the Opposition, and as soon as the House closed he allowed this constitution destroyer and outrager to place two monkey-like political poltroons in the Legislative Council, and then accepted those two political moralists as his advisers and ministers of the Crown, while he knew right well that had the people a say respecting the two positions—as they undoubtedly had—that they would not secure enough votes to save their nomination fees.

Governor Davidson is just as guilty of tearing up the constitution and outraging the decisions of the electorate as Sir Edward Morris is, and consequently the Toilers have lost confidence in him.

An unidentified survivor of the *Newfoundland* disaster is carried by stretcher. The Commission of Enquiry would later recommend ways to make the seal hunt safer. *MHA, PF-345.018*

The Commission of Enquiry into the Sealing Disasters of 1914 was an unprecedented opportunity to change one of Newfoundland's core industries for the better. It had the time and resources to thoroughly examine the seal hunt's practices; it had a much broader mandate than the two enquiries that had preceded it (the Magisterial Enquiry into the *Newfoundland* disaster and the Marine Court of Enquiry into the *Southern Cross*); and legislators were under significant public pressure to enact its recommendations.

There were three commissioners: Supreme Court Judges William H. Horwood, George H. Emerson, and George M. Johnson. They heard from 52 witnesses and examined logbooks, telegraph messages, hospital reports, and other supporting documentation. They also had access to the already substantial evidence collected by the two previous investigations—the Magisterial Enquiry into the *Newfoundland* disaster and the Marine Court of Enquiry into the disappearance of the *Southern Cross*.

On February 24, 1915, Commissioners Horwood and

Emerson submitted a joint report to the government, followed by Johnson's minority report three days later. Although Johnson dismissed the disasters as an "Act of God, and in the circumstances inevitable," Horwood and Emerson disagreed. They firmly placed the blame on human error and found that the *Newfoundland* disaster in particular could have been easily avoided.

Horwood and Emerson cited two primary causes. The first was Westbury Kean's decision to send his men so far from the ship that they could not return for the night. The second was Abram Kean's "grave error of judgment" in leaving the men on the ice without arranging to pick them up later or send another steamer to find them. Tuff was also criticized for accepting Abram Kean's orders without question. However, the report was directed more at preventing future disasters than at doling out punishment, and no charges were laid.

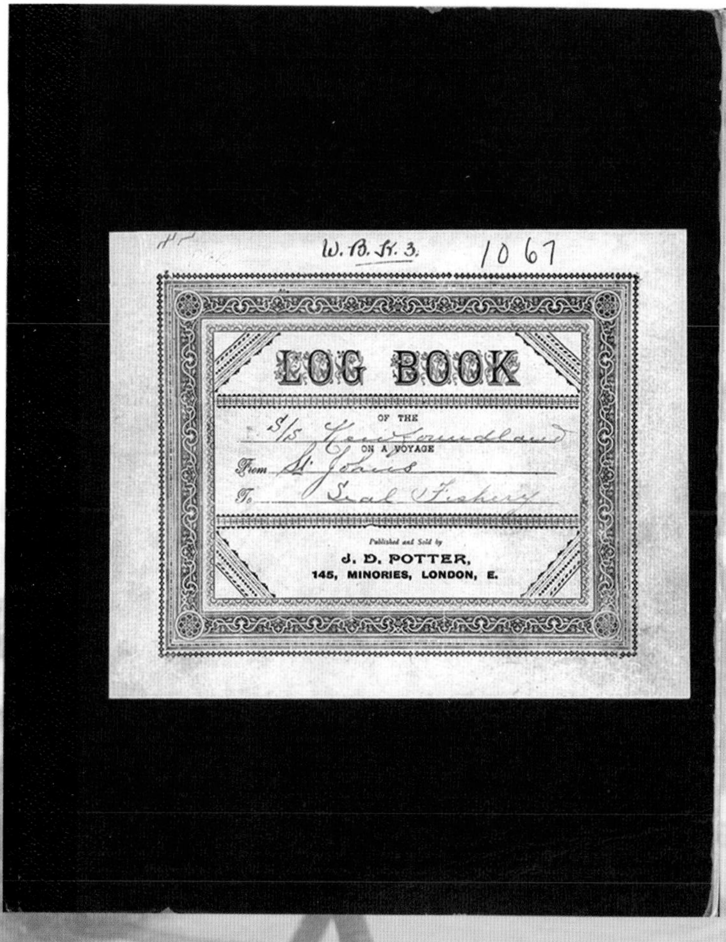

The *Newfoundland*'s logbook was one of many pieces of evidence the commissioners examined. *The Rooms Provincial Archives Division, GN 121-51*

Capt. W. Kean Believes
Wireless Telegraphy
Would Have Saved Life

Captain Westbury Kean.
ASCD, Coll. 203 5.57.001; Daily Mail, April 9, 1914

The three commissioners made many recommendations aimed at improving worker safety. Captains should never order their men so far from the vessel that they could not return within one hour after sunset, nor should they ask sealers to hunt before sunrise and after sunset. The shipowner (i.e., merchant firm) should be held accountable for any work-related deaths and injuries by providing financial compensation to the sealer or his dependants. As a precaution, steamers should sound their whistles at regular intervals if any crewmembers were on the ice in fog, mist, snow, or darkness.

The commissioners also recommended that steamers carry competent medical personnel and that someone be placed in charge of inspecting the sealers before they left the vessel to ensure that they were properly dressed and carrying an adequate supply of food. No vessel should depart for the hunt before being approved by a qualified inspector and all steamers should receive wireless weather reports three times a day. They applauded the government's recent Act making wireless equipment mandatory.

After the Commission

MR. COAKER'S LOG

The voyage is ended. It occupied four weeks wanting one day. I enjoyed it very much and value highly the experiences and observations of the trip, some of which I shall always remember with pleasure. I advise all who can to take this trip. It is impossible to know what the seal hunt is like unless one sees it for oneself. Such ships as the *Stephano* and *Florizel* should offer trips to a limited number of passengers at a reasonable cost, say $50, when I believe many would gladly avail of the opportunity to see things as they are.

EVERYTHING INTERESTING

To the beginner everything is interesting from the time port is left until the young seals are cut up. I was treated with kindness and respect throughout by officers and men, and I avail of this opportunity to thank Captain Barbour for his unfailing courtesy and consideration while on board. I also thank the officers and crew for the many acts of kindness shown me.

The stewards were obliging and courteous. My mess mates were Dr. Bunting, Chief Engineer Ledingham, Second Engineer Black, Mate Keough, and the third and fourth engineer in turn. Many a ten-minute chat we had over the mess table. Dr. Bunting is an intelligent and genial companion and all on board respected him. I have seldom met an equal more reasonable in discussion and moderate in his opinions.

Chief Ledingham and Second Black are both intelligent and genial chaps and it was a pleasure to converse with them.

FOGGY COMING IN

Very foggy approaching the land. Made in below Sugar Loaf. Arrived about 8 p.m. Dr. Campbell [the medical port quarantine officer for St. John's] gave the ship a clean bill of health and kindly offered me a passage ashore in the Customs boat. The first thing I did was to read Monday's *Daily Mail*, which contained such a splendid account of the disaster, and the *Evening Telegram* of Thursday, which contained the evidence of several witnesses regarding the disaster.

All that sailed in the *Nascopie* returned in good health. The voyage was ended and many thankful hearts exclaimed "Thank God" for our safe return and sound health.

This diary was begun with the intention of publishing it in the *Advocate* Xmas Number, accompanied with illustrations. That idea I will forego in view of the awful disaster which overtook the *Newfoundland*'s crew. I therefore publish it now for the information of the Sons of Toil, in order to show the conditions as they existed, which in a major degree has a bearing upon the calamity that has come upon our country.

The Newfoundland House of Assembly, 1914. New legislation was passed in the wake of the *Newfoundland* and *Southern Cross* disasters to make the sealing industry safer. *The Rooms Provincial Archives Division, C 1-207*

The government was under intense pressure from the public, press, and the Fishermen's Protective Union to act on the Commission of Enquiry's recommendations. Even before the report was completed, legislators had made wireless sets mandatory on sealing vessels. They introduced many more regulations in the next two years.

In 1915, the government created a Permanent Marine Disasters Fund for the families of dead or injured sealers. Later legislation would require merchant firms to financially compensate the dependants of anyone injured or killed while working at the floes for one of their vessels.

The 1916 Act Respecting the Seal Fishery implemented many of the commission's recommendations. Ice captains could no longer order their men to hunt after dark or in stormy weather. If sealers were on the ice after dark, vessels were required to sound their whistle regularly. Steamers also had to be equipped with emergency signal rockets and lifeboats. Fines for each offence ranged from $100 to $500. A new board of examiners was also created to check the qualifications of potential new ice captains, master watches, and second hands.

The new legislation was a step forward, but several factors undermined it. The government did not create any independent regulatory agencies able to properly enforce the new rules and police the industry. Inspectors were usually paid out of the hunt's profits, which placed their impartiality into question. The First World War also siphoned attention away from the hunt and weakened the government's ability and willingness to introduce new sealing laws or strongly enforce the existing ones.

However, the war also did much to increase safety at the floes. Soon after hostilities erupted, the merchant firms handed over many of the sealing fleet's steel-hulled steamers to the war effort. The wooden vessels no longer had to keep up with the more powerful iron-clads and less competition at the floes resulted in increased safety.

Never again was there a sealing disaster that came close to those of 1914.

Seal oil being extracted at the St. John's merchant firm Job Brothers and Company, 1902. *MHA, PF-316.016*

Between 1915 and 1916, the steel-hulled steamers *Bellaventure* (pictured here), *Beothic*, *Adventure*, and *Bonaventure* were sold to Russia, which was allied with Britain and France during the First World War. *MHA, PF-055.2-H32*

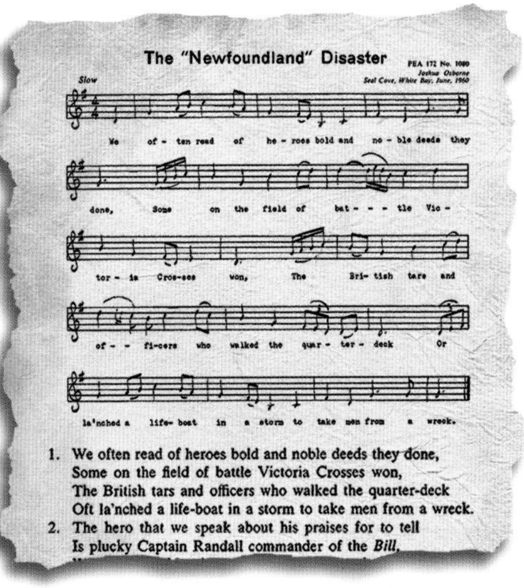

From *Songs of the Newfoundland Outports*, by Kenneth Peacock, 1965.

MR. COAKER'S LOG

These notes will be reproduced in the Xmas Number of the *Advocate* accompanied with some very interesting cuts, illustrating the incidents referred to herein, as I have taken some fifty photos during the trip.

MEALS SERVED OUT

The men's cook reports having served out to the crew the following meals during the voyage: Beans served 14 mornings, brewse and watered fish with pork dressing 13 mornings, soft bread every second morning, 12 hot dinners served consisting of beef, pork, potatoes, plain and plum pudding, and on Sunday fresh beef or canned roast beef in addition; pea soup with potatoes, turnip, onions, and dumplins served for dinner eight days; seal and other soups served for dinner seven days—thus a dinner was cooked every day. On Sunday canned beef and apple jam was served for tea in addition to sweet bread and tea, and the tea on Sundays was sugared and milked. Potatoes, turnips, and meat were given out to the crew when required, which the men cooked themselves for supper. Three pounds of soft bread being found insufficient, the amount was increased to five pounds per man per week. Warm soup was served to the men when coming off the ice, and if any of the sealers fell in they were served with a grog [a shot of liquor] when they reached the ship. I fear a few of them when near the ship occasionally managed to get somewhat wet in order to qualify for a grog, but the steward soon caught on.

Capt. Randell, of the *Bellaventure*, pushed through well, and kept close to the larger ships during the whole voyage. Especially was he persistent in forcing along enroute to the seals and entered the patch in company with the other three foremost ships—*Nascopie*, *Stephano*, and *Beothic*.

From reports made by sealers, the conditions and food on board of the *Erik*, *Ranger*, and *Bloodhound* could not be much worse. The owners must be blamed, for the men speak in the highest terms of Capt. Jesse Winsor and Kenneth Knee, who have done their best for the men. The facilities were not provided and No. 2 flour was supplied for bread, and no cook could make good bread from bad flour and no cooking facilities.

Captains Joe Kean, John Parsons, and Randell are well spoken of by their crews, and we believe they did all in their power to live up to the sealing laws.

An Enduring Legacy

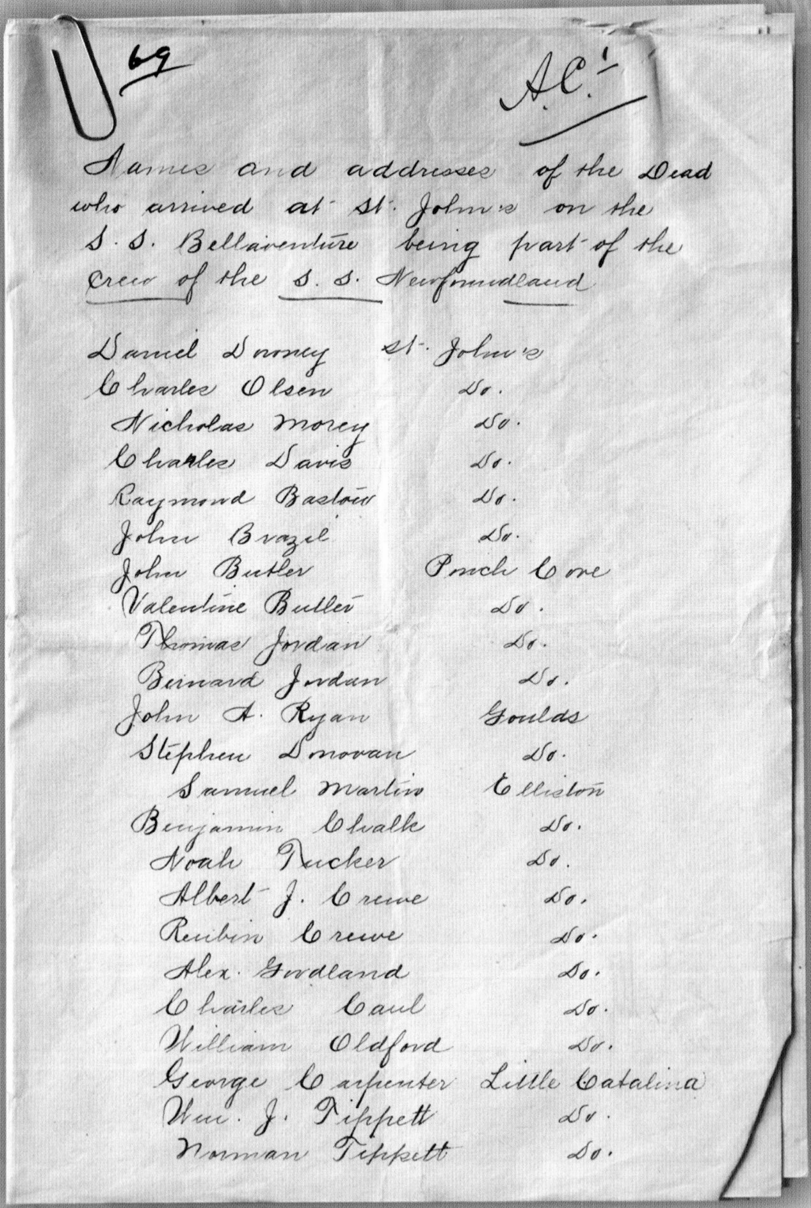
69

A.C.

Names and addresses of the Dead who arrived at St. John's on the S. S. Bellaventure being part of the crew of the S. S. Newfoundland

Daniel Dorney	St. John's
Charles Olsen	Do.
Nicholas Morey	Do.
Charles Davis	Do.
Raymond Bastow	Do.
John Brazil	Do.
John Butler	Pouch Cove
Valentine Butler	Do.
Thomas Jordan	Do.
Bernard Jordan	Do.
John A. Ryan	Goulds
Stephen Donovan	Do.
Samuel Martin	Elliston
Benjamin Chalk	Do.
Noah Tucker	Do.
Albert J. Crewe	Do.
Reubin Crewe	Do.
Alex. Gordland	Do.
Charles Caul	Do.
William Oldford	Do.
George Carpenter	Little Catalina
Wm. J. Pippett	Do.
Norman Tippett	Do.

The tragedy of the spring of 1914 was seared into Newfoundland's collective consciousness. This is particularly true of the *Newfoundland* disaster, which tells a story of human endurance, courage, and heartbreak. It is about people who fought for their lives in a hostile environment and a ruthless industry. In the decades since, it has been told and retold in photographs, songs, books, art, and film.

In the 1960s, visual artist David Blackwood produced 50 etchings based on the disaster. Called *The Lost Party*, it is one of the most famous and critically acclaimed series of thematically linked prints in Canadian history. In an interview with *Canadian Forum* in May 1978, Blackwood emphasized the cultural significance of the seal hunt, saying it "might well be the only Canadian mythology existing outside our native cultures. Contrary to what some people would have us believe, it is not the building of the Canadian Pacific

David Blackwood's etching on the cover of *Death on the Ice*.
Used by permission of Doubleday Canada

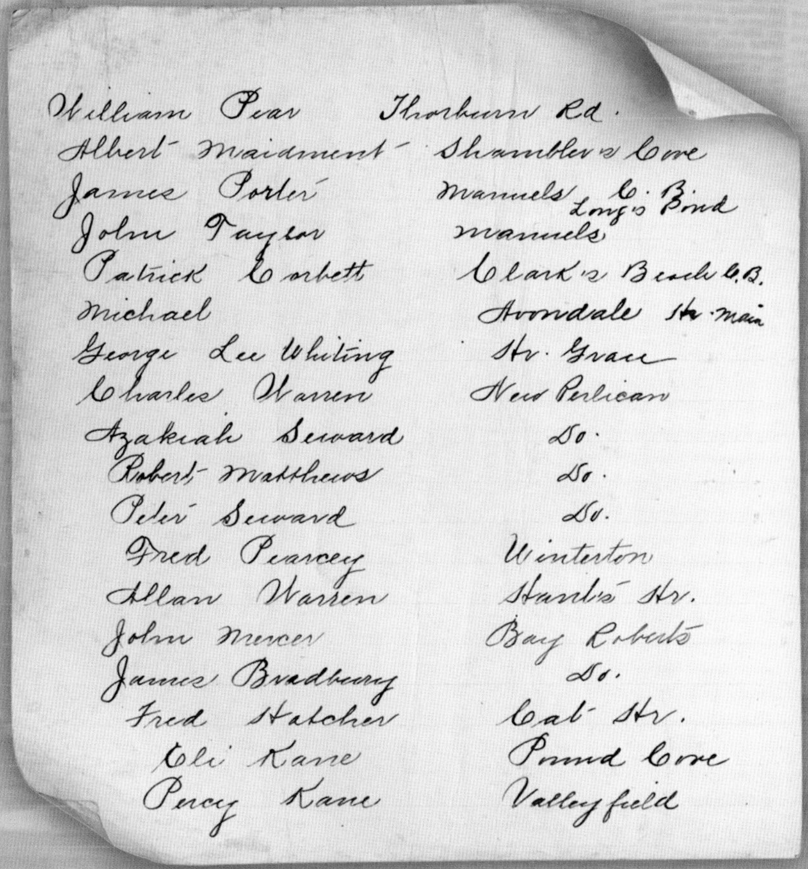

William Pear	Thorburn Rd.
Albert Maidment	Shambler's Cove
James Porter	Manuels C. B.
John Tayler	Manuels Long's Pond
Patrick Corbett	Clark's Beach C.B.
Michael	Avondale Hr. Main
George Lee Whiting	Hr. Grace
Charles Warren	New Perlican
Azakiah Seward	Do.
Robert Matthews	Do.
Peter Seward	Do.
Fred Pearcey	Winterton
Allan Warren	Hant's Hr.
John Mercer	Bay Roberts
James Bradbury	Do.
Fred Hatcher	Cat Hr.
Eli Kane	Pound Cove
Percy Kane	Valleyfield

Railway. The lore of Newfoundland is full of very rich imagery."

In 1972, Cassie Brown published her seminal book, *Death on the Ice*. She meticulously researched the disaster by interviewing survivors and by studying court and government records, archival documents, newspapers, and scores of photographs. Much of her research is now housed at the Archives and Special Collections Division on the Memorial University campus. Brown's book was a bestseller and taught in schools. It was one of the first times that Newfoundland and Labrador students were given the opportunity to learn about their own history and to study the work of a local writer.

In 1991, the National Film Board of Canada produced the documentary *"I Just Didn't Want to Die": The 1914* Newfoundland *Sealing Disaster*. Later that decade, the disaster figured prominently in Wayne Johnston's critically acclaimed work of historical fiction, *The Colony of Unrequited Dreams*. More recently, it was the basis for a series of paintings by John McDonald, *You Don't Know Cold*, which showed at The Rooms Provincial Art Gallery in 2012.

To commemorate the disaster's 100th anniversary, a Sealers' Memorial and Interpretation Centre will open in 2014 at Elliston, a historic sealing community in Bonavista Bay. One of the site's centrepieces will be a life-sized bronze statue depicting Reuben Crewe and his son Albert John. The pair froze to death in each other's arms while stranded on the ice. They were two of the eight men from Elliston who died that spring.

Although no longer a part of our living memory, the 1914 sealing disasters resonate in Newfoundland and Labrador. The *Newfoundland* disaster has given rise to some of the finest and most important works to come from this province, and it remains a compelling topic of study for artists and scholars. The disasters are still taught in the province's schools and remembered at its museums, galleries, archives, and cultural sites.

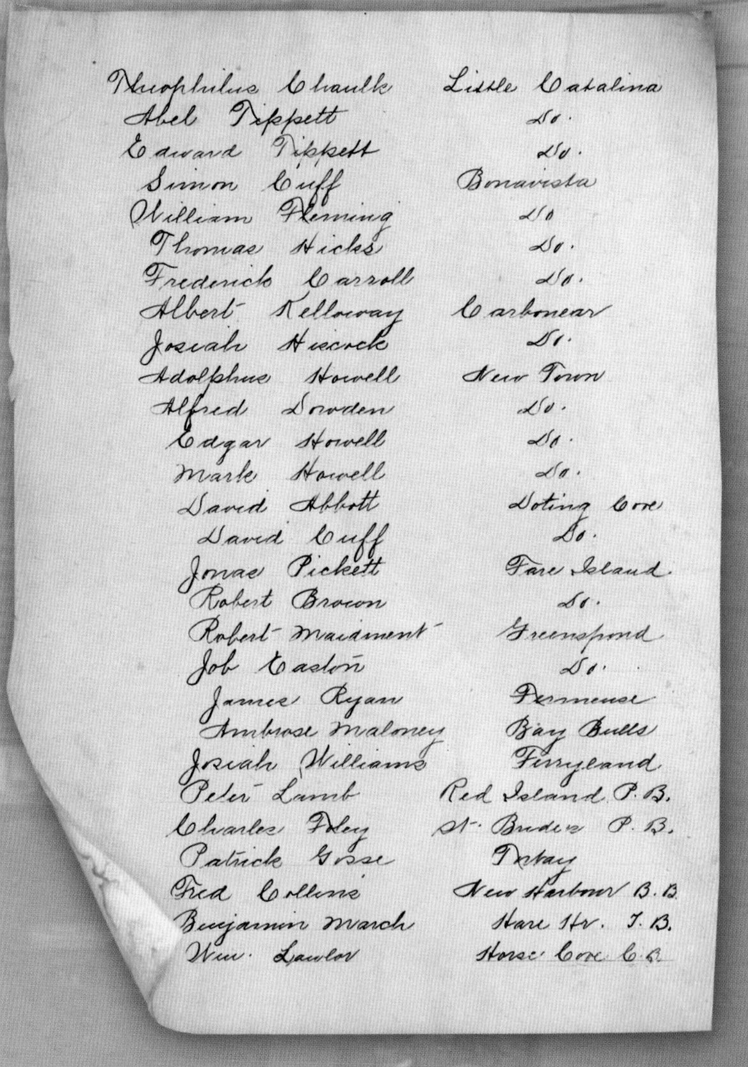

Theophilus Chaulk	Little Catalina
Abel Tippett	Do.
Edward Tippett	Do.
Simon Cuff	Bonavista
William Fleming	Do.
Thomas Hicks	Do.
Frederick Carroll	Do.
Albert Kelloway	Carbonear
Josiah Hiscock	Do.
Adolphus Howell	New Town
Alfred Dowden	Do.
Edgar Howell	Do.
Mark Howell	Do.
David Abbott	Doting Cove
David Cuff	Do.
Jonas Pickett	Fair Island
Robert Brown	Do.
Robert Maidment	Greenspond
Job Easton	Do.
James Ryan	Fermeuse
Ambrose Maloney	Bay Bulls
Josiah Williams	Ferryland
Peter Lamb	Red Island P.B.
Charles Foley	St. Brides P.B.
Patrick Gosse	Torbay
Fred Collins	New Harbour B.B.
Benjamin March	Hare Hr. T.B.
Wm. Lawlor	Horse Cove C.B.

List of the bodies brought back to Newfoundland by the *Bellaventure*. Eight bodies were never recovered: Henry Dowden, Philip Holoway, James Howell, Henry Jordan, David Locke, Ezra Melendy, Art Mouland, and Mike Murrary. *The Rooms Provincial Archives Division, GN 121-46*

Additional Credits

Chapter 1: Invitation to the Ice
Background images: MHA, PF-315.104, PF-315.124
Image of Coaker, far right, from William Coaker, *The History of the Fishermen's Protective Union of Newfoundland* (St. John's: Union Publishing Company, Ltd., 1920)

Chapter 2: The Fleet Departs
Background images: MHA, PF-001.1-J37b, PF-001.1-A07

Chapter 3: Into the Floes
Background images: The Rooms Provincial Archives Division, VA 44-17; MHA, PF-315.234
Map courtesy NL Heritage Website
Pullout: ASCD, Coll. 307 15.01.042

Chapter 4: Ice Everywhere
Background images: MHA, PF-118.008, PF-001.1-P41; ASCD, Coll. 203 7.01.037
Pullout: ASCD, Coll. 307 15.01.034

Chapter 5: The Vocabulary of the Hunt
Background images: MHA, PF-118.013, PF-320.007

Chapter 6: First Day on the Ice
Background images: MHA, PF-323.042, PF-118.011

Chapter 7: 1898 *Greenland* Disaster
Background images: MHA, PF-118.021, PF-118.017
Pullout: *Evening Telegram*, March 28, 1898

Chapter 8: A List of Crew
Background images: MHA, PF-118.009; The Rooms Provincial Archives Division, VA 137-56

Chapter 9: Nothing but Risk and Peril
Background images: MHA, PF-325.022; *Evening Herald*, April 5, 1914

Chapter 10: The Ice Captains
Background images: MHA, PF-320.004, PF-118.012

Chapter 11: The Spoils of the Hunt
Background images: MHA, PF-315.064, PF-118.018
Pullout: MHA, MF-0139

Chapter 12: Leisure Time
Background images: MHA, PF-321.025, PF-286.026
"Come All Ye Jolly Ice-Hunters," from *Old Time Songs and Poetry of Newfoundland* (St. John's: Gerald S. Doyle Ltd., 1927)

Chapter 13: Other Kinds of Sealers
Background images: MHA, PF-325.095, PF-055.2-W82, PF-325.114, PF-325.125
Drawing by W.G.R. Hind, from Henry Y. Hind, *Explorations in the Interior of the Labrador Peninsula* (Portugal Cove-St. Philip's, NL: Boulder Publications, 2007)

Chapter 15: On the Eve of Disaster
Background images: MHA, PF-118.003, PF-118.019, PF-320.002
Pullout: The Rooms Provincial Archives Division, GN 121-48

Chapter 16: Ordered Overboard
Background image spread 1: MHA, PF-118.016
Background images spread 2: MHA, PF-118.021; ASCD, Coll. 115 16.04.099
Model ship: Photo by John H. Andela
Pullout: The Rooms Provincial Archives Division, GN 121-49

Chapter 17: Second Day on the Ice
Background images spread 1: MHA, PF-055.2-T56, PF-286.034
Background images spread 2: ASCD, Coll. 115 16.04.040, Coll. 115 16.04.036
Pullout: The Rooms Provincial Archives Division, GN 121-50

Chapter 18: Rescue
Background images spread 1: ASCD, Coll. 115 16.04.036, Coll. 115 16.04.065; MHA, PF-345.011
Pullout: The Rooms Provincial Archives Division, GN 121-51

Chapter 19: Reaction
Background image spread 1: ASCD, Coll. 203 8.01.005
Background image spread 2: MHA, PF-345.012
Pullout: The Rooms Provincial Archives Division, GN 121-49, Despatches 1 and 7

Chapter 20: Landing Survivors
Background images spread 1: ASCD, Coll. 115 16.04.044; MHA, PF-345.015
Background image spread 2: *Daily Mail*, April 6, 1914

Chapter 21: Mourning and Mutiny
Background images: City of St. John's Archives, 1.42.001; MHA, PF-315.093
Envelope photo: MHA, PF-318.030
Pullout: The Rooms Provincial Archives Division, GN 121-46

Chapter 23: Mourning the *Southern Cross*
Background image: MHA, PF-315.094
"The Southern Cross," from *Old Time Songs and Poetry of Newfoundland* (St. John's: Gerald S. Doyle Ltd., 1927)

Chapter 24: A Call for Change
Background images: MHA, PF-315.159, PF-315.001

Chapter 25: Coaker's Campaign
Background images: MHA, PF-315.018, PF-315.085

Chapter 26: Commission of Enquiry
Background images: MHA, PF-315.019, PF-345.007

Chapter 27: After the Commission
Background images: MHA, PF-316.023, PF-345.006

Acknowledgements

This book draws heavily upon archival documents to tell its story. It is fortunate, therefore, that I live in a city filled with knowledgeable and big-hearted archivists, librarians, and historians. I owe thanks to many people.

I am especially grateful to Heather Wareham and the Maritime History Archive (MHA) at Memorial University. Without her knowledge, advice, and generosity, this book would not have been possible. Many of the images contained in these pages came from the MHA's extensive and exceptional collection. My time spent there examining photographs, reading old newspapers, and studying crew agreements, diaries, and other documents greatly informed my understanding of the topic and the time period.

I am grateful to Vince Walsh, coordinator of the Newfoundland and Labrador Heritage Website at the MHA, for both his help with this book and for employing me as a writer and researcher since 2006. My work at the website has given me the knowledge to write this book.

Thanks also to the staff at other archives, libraries, and repositories at Memorial University where I did research. The Archives and Special Collections Division was crucial to this book and I would like to thank Linda White, Paulette Noseworthy, and Colleen Quigley for their help and patience. The Centre for Newfoundland Studies (CNS) was of tremendous help to me as well, and my deep thanks go to Joan Ritcey and the other wonderful people who work there. Many thanks go to Suzanne Power and to those connected with the English Language Research Centre (ELRC) for letting me reproduce word files from the *Dictionary of Newfoundland English* Collection. Also at Memorial University, I would like to thank the Digital Archives Initiative (DAI) and Don Walsh.

Off campus, I did significant work at The Rooms Provincial Archives, which has an excellent collection and such a lovely reading room. I owe a large debt of gratitude to the many people who work there. The City of St. John's Archives was invaluable, and I extend thanks to Helen Miller and Alanna Wicks for generously sharing their knowledge.

My deep thanks go to Dr. Sean Cadigan of Memorial University's History Department for reviewing this manuscript. I am grateful for the time and advice he gave to me so freely.

Other individuals and publishers I would like to thank for giving me access to images or documents from their collections include Marjorie Doyle and the Doyle family; model-ship builder John Andela; and Doubleday Canada.

Warm thanks go to my editor and dear friend Stephanie Porter for her endless support, patience, knowledge, and insight; to Gavin Will of Boulder Publications, who helped to conceive of this volume; to Mona Atari, a magician among graphic designers; and to Iona Bulgin, the best and most rigorous copy editor I have ever met.

And thanks go to Phillip for his constant support.

Further Reading

Baker, Melvin. "Document: President Coaker's Log of His Trip to the Ice Floe Last Spring in S.S. *Nascopie* [1914]." *Newfoundland and Labrador Studies* 25.2 (2010): 217-252.

Brown, Cassie. *Death on the Ice: The Great Newfoundland Sealing Disaster of 1914.* Toronto: Doubleday Canada, 1972.

Cadigan, Sean T. *Death on Two Fronts: National Tragedies and the Fate of Democracy in Newfoundland, 1914-34.* Toronto: Penguin Canada, 2013.

England, George Allan. *Vikings of the Ice, Being the Log of a Tenderfoot on the Great Newfoundland Seal Hunt.* Garden City, NY: Doubleday, Page & Co., 1924.

Gray, Doug. *R.M.S.* Nascopie: *Ship of the North.* Ottawa: Golden Dog Press, 1997.

Greene, William Howe. *The Wooden Walls among the Ice Floes, Telling the Romance of the Newfoundland Seal Fishery.* London: Hutchinson & Co. Ltd., 1933.

Harrington, Michael. *Goin' to the Ice: Offbeat History of the Newfoundland Sealfishery.* St. John's: Harry Cuff Publications, 1986.

Hogan, Peter J. *The Disaster Spring: Politics of the Newfoundland Seal Fishery, 1908-1919.* Hons. Diss. (B.A.), Memorial University of Newfoundland, 2009.

Kean, Abram. *Old and Young Ahead.* St. John's: Flanker Press, 2000.

McDonald, Ian. *Coaker the Reformer: A Brief Biographical Introduction.* St. John's: Memorial University of Newfoundland, 1975.

McDonald, Ian and J.K. Hiller. *"To Each His Own": William Coaker and the Fishermen's Protective Union in Newfoundland Politics, 1908-1925.* St. John's: Institute of Social and Economic Research, Memorial University of Newfoundland, 1987.

Mowat, Farley and David Blackwood. *Wake of the Great Sealers.* Boston: Little, Brown, 1973.

O'Flaherty, Patrick. *Lost Country: The Rise and Fall of Newfoundland, 1843-1933.* St. John's: Long Beach Press, 2005.

Doyle, Gerald S. *Old Time Songs and Poetry of Newfoundland: Songs of the People from the Days of Our Forefathers.* St. John's: G.S. Doyle, 1940.

Peacock, Kenneth. *Songs of the Newfoundland Outports.* Ottawa: National Museum of Canada, 1965.

Report of the Commission of Enquiry into the Sealing Disasters of 1914. St. John's: Newfoundland Government, 1915.

Ryan, Shannon. *The Ice Hunters: A History of Newfoundland Sealing to 1914.* St. John's: Breakwater, 1994.

Ryan, Shannon, ed. *Chafe's Sealing Book: A Statistical Record of the Newfoundland Steamer Seal Fishery, 1863-1941.* St. John's: Breakwater, 1989.

Ryan, Shannon and Larry Small. *Haulin' Rope and Gaff: Songs and Poetry in the History of the Newfoundland Seal Fishery.* St. John's: Breakwater, 1978.

Ryan, Shannon, Cater Andrews, and Martha Drake. *Seals and Sealers: A Pictorial History of the Newfoundland Seal Fishery Based on the Cater Andrews Collection.* St. John's: Breakwater, 1987.

Story, G.M., W.J. Kirwin, and J.D.A. Widdowson. *Dictionary of Newfoundland English.* Toronto: University of Toronto Press, 1982.

Primary Sources

Cassie Brown Collection, Coll. 115, Archives and Special Collections Division, Memorial University.

Dictionary of Newfoundland English Collection, English Language Research Centre, Memorial University.

Marine Court of Enquiry into the Loss of the SS *Southern Cross* fonds, GN 2/5, File 92-D, The Rooms Provincial Archives.

Royal Commission of Enquiry into the Sealing Disasters of 1914 fonds, GN 121, The Rooms Provincial Archives.